ANOTHER VIEW:
TRACING THE FOREIGN IN LITERARY TRANSLATION

Another View:
Tracing the Foreign in Literary Translation

EDUARD STOKLOSINSKI

DALKEY ARCHIVE PRESS
Champaign / London / Dublin

Please see *Rights and Permissions* on page 213
for individual credits

First edition, 2014
Second Printing, 2015
All rights reserved

Library of Congress Cataloging-in-Publication Data

Stoklosinski, Eduard. Another view : tracing the
foreign in literary translation / Eduard Stoklosinski.
-- First edition.
pages cm
ISBN 978-1-62897-060-9
1. Translating and interpreting. 2. Language
and languages--Foreign elements. I. Title.
PN241.S742 2014
418'.04--dc23
2014010843

Partially funded by a grant from the Illinois Arts
Council, a state agency

The author wishes to extend his special thanks for
the support of Associate Professor David Brooks and
the unwavering encouragement and commitment of
Ruth Anne Balint

www.dalkeyarchive.com
Cover: design and composition by Mikhail Iliatov

Für Emil, das Licht über meinem Kopf

Contents

Preface

The present volume was inspired by an exhibition at the Goethe Institute in Budapest in late 2008. At that time, the downstairs café in the Goethe building in Ráday Utca featured an inconspicuous photo and book display entitled *Der andere Blick*, "the other view," which portrayed and promoted recent book releases of German authors from a non-German cultural background. Some of the writers presented there, Marica Bodrožić or Dimitré Dinev for example, were comparatively new arrivals on the German literary stage; others, at least within contemporary German literature, were well-established: Terézia Mora, Yoko Tawada, Feridun Zaimoglu, and, of course, Herta Müller, who rather unexpectedly won the Nobel Prize for Literature a year later.

What I found immediately engaging about these authors and their writing was the range of cultural topographies and dispositions these works suggested, the allure of narrative materializing at the interchange of different languages. The assembled texts promised an encounter with the intercultural margin Jamal Tuschick in *Neueste Deutsche Literatur* passionately referred to as "*Träger wichtiger Zukunftsinformationen*" (carriers of important future information) (84)[1]; they represented a collision, a confluence of place and language, transposed from a familiar frame of reference and subjected to a foreign frame of mind, a motion pertaining to the realm of literary translation.

As a literary translator working in a second language, I had been interested for quite some time in prose by authors of non-native backgrounds, and I became intrigued by the theoretical implications of a translation project encompassing second-language literature in second-language translation and the challenge of existing tenets, in particular readability and directionality, within translation theory. I began looking for traces of the authors' non-German language origins that had formed and informed their writing in German, the framing of the foreign residue these writers worked with and how their different cultural background collided with and imprinted itself in their

[1] All translated quotes, unless otherwise indicated, are the work of the author.

writing language. Sifting through these texts, I was largely indifferent to questions of language mastery, the subjugation of an "object" for the writer's purpose; what interested me was how the other, in this case German language, facilitated and furthered their writing, how it afforded these authors a particular textuality. I was especially curious to discover how their perspectives and textures might manifest themselves in translation.

This project examines the relevance of directionality in the translation of literary texts by looking at the significance of the "foreign" as an integral motif and constituent in writing. Exploring the ramifications of translating into a "foreign," non-native language prompts a questioning, a closer evaluation of traditional norms of fluidity, naturalness or coherence prevalent in literary translation practice, which coincide with the entrenched dogmas of mother tongue and native speaker. The common misconception by the Anglophone reader that the translation *is* the original text (Venuti "Mémoires") and therefore void of any traces, unaffected by its foreign origin, urged me to think about aspects of the reciprocal relationship between writing and language and translating.

I have refrained from presenting an overarching systematic framework or model for translating literature into a foreign language. To subject and reduce the act of translating to prescriptive constructs is a trivial undertaking, as translation is bound by a convergence of circumstances and motivations: the particular aesthetics of the original text; the translator's political and cultural background and literary affiliations and sensibilities; the place and time of writing and translating; the standards, rationales and dictates that impact on the creation and production of the original text and the translation. Instead, I seek to reflect on current objectives determining the face of literary translation and the circumstances that have contributed to the entrenchment of these norms and applications. For this purpose, I situate this inquiry in cultural, historical and literary contexts that had or have decisive impacts on the current praxis in literary translation. My reading of texts as a translator and the resulting consideration of language in the writing process have been influenced by the *Auseinandersetzung*, my engagement with these questions.

Introduction

The Experience of the Foreign in the Original

> Dichter schreiben nicht nur, wie viele andere, die schreiben
> und reden, weil sie glauben, dass sie etwas zu sagen haben,
> sondern ebensosehr, damit sie etwas zu sagen haben, etwas, das
> ihnen die Sprache, der sie es ablauschen, zuträgt und erst zu
> sagen ermöglicht.   —Hans-Jost Frey (40)

> Poets do not write simply because, like many others who write
> and talk, they think they have something to say; they write in
> equal measure so that they have something to say, something
> the language they listen in on provides and enables them to say.

The initial manifestations of contemporary intercultural writing in Germany can be traced back to the 1970s and '80s. *Ausländerliteratur*, or literature of foreigners, under which these texts were lumped together, was a problematic and generalizing term that homogenized a range of diverse texts, authors, backgrounds and circumstances. The label is, however, relatively useful in distinguishing the collective experience of these authors and the sociopolitical context in which their writing developed from individual, peripatetic writers who, independently and of their own volition, have left their place of origin for a different cultural milieu to continue and further their writing ambitions. Less common among the latter kind are writers who have, apart from their place, also left behind their language of origin and have decided, by preference or necessity, to write in another, or in more than one language: Samuel Beckett, for instance, wrote and translated his later work in French; Ödön von Horvath, Joseph Conrad and Milan Kundera are other examples of writers who worked in second or third languages.

The first prominent émigré writer of German literature was Adalbert von Chamisso, after whom the Adalbert-von-Chamisso-Preis was named, a unique award established in 1985 and presented to German writers whose mother tongue and cultural background are non-German. Chamisso left France in 1792 as a young boy with his patrician family following the confiscation of the family estate by revolutionary troops. Four years later, the Chamissos settled in Berlin, where they found refuge and acceptance at the Prussian court and among the French Huguenot community. Chamisso visited the *Französische Gymnasium* and began to study German, the language in which he would later write his famous novel *Peter Schlemihls wundersame Geschichte.*

Chamisso's plight and the migration history of the Huguenots in Berlin at the end of the seventeenth century can be read as a precursor to the migration experience that would unfold in the same city three hundred years later. The promise of a better life—that is to say, economic and to a lesser extent political motives—led to the migration of 2.5 million people to West Germany in the 1960s and '70s, mainly from southern European countries, the largest migration program in modern Germany's history. These euphemistically or sardonically named *Gastarbeiter* (guest workers) were recruited by the West German government to sell their labour power in the booming postwar economy, although successive governments and policymakers during that time would not tire to proclaim, paradoxically, that *Deutschland ist kein Einwanderungsland* (Germany is not an immigrant country) (Herbert 250). The convenient official reasoning was that the *Gastarbeiter* would return to their homeland once their labour was no longer required. In his diaries, the Swiss author Max Frisch (12) summed up this absurd official posturing in a laconic, trenchant note: "*Ein kleines Herrenvolk sieht sich in Gefahr: man hat Arbeitskräfte gerufen, und es kommen Menschen*" (a small master race feels threatened: they called for a workforce, and human beings arrived).

The migrants at that time predominantly came from rural backgrounds. They encountered a highly industrialized economy, although the working and living conditions they found themselves in were rather less advanced: Menial, dirty and dangerous work and substandard housing were the norm. Exposed to a foreign, forbidding culture and language, the migrants were frequently confronted with resentment and discrimination. Many migrants felt isolated and alienated from their new environment and also, in a sense, from the life they had left behind. In their manifesto *Literatur der Betroffenheit*, the authors Franco Biondi and Rafik Shami sketched the initial dimension of this encounter:

> Die Gastarbeiter kommen meist aus südlichen Ländern, sie kommen aus ländlichen Gebieten und sind von der dortigen kulturellen Entwicklung geprägt. Sie kommen hierher und erleben einen Bruch, denn sie werden in eine festgefügte, auf einem anderen Stand der Entwicklung sich befindende Kultur hineingeworfen ... In dieser Phase versucht der Gastarbeiter zuerst mit seiner Umwelt und seiner Identität klarzuwerden. Es ist ein umwälzender Prozess, durch den ... ein Gastarbeiter, auch mit geringer Schulbildung, zum ersten Mal begreift, wie wichtig es ist, seine Erfahrung zu vermitteln. (124)

> The guest workers mainly come from southern European countries, they come from rural areas and are defined by the cultural development there. They come here and experience a rupture because they are thrown into a culture which is at a different stage of development... In this situation the *Gastarbeiter* tries first of all to come to terms with the environment and his identity. It is a sweeping process, in which ... a *Gastarbeiter* even with little formal education understands for the first time how important it is to communicate his experience.

For some migrants, coming to terms with their mental and physical dislocation was to express, to put into words the situation they faced; they began to write, letters, diaries or poems, texts in which they recorded and documented their experiences and examined their predicament. Some were accomplished writers, others took up the pen for the first time. Gino Chiellino (*Literatur* 20), an influential figure of migrant literature in West Germany at that time, suggested that writing at this stage had to be understood as a substitute for a failed or absent verbal communication: "*Das geschriebene Blatt wird zum Partner in der Isolation, gegen die Isolation. Der Schreibende kann mit ihm, durch es re-*

den, das Sprechen wieder lernen" (The written page becomes a partner in the isolation, against isolation. The writer is able to communicate with it, communicate through it, learn to speak again).

At the same time, however, the physical and emotional dislocation exacerbated the perception of an impenetrable language environment, attempts at finding a voice often resulted in a loss of language, being excluded, outside, invisible. This loss of language represents, in particular for established writers, a loss of self, a severing of past and present, as the Kurdish writer Mehmed Uzun reflected on his Swedish exile:

> I lost my mother tongue, my motherland, as Albert Camus puts it, my most sacred possession. My mother tongue suddenly became useless, meaningless, and a burden. It stopped protecting me; it stopped giving me a sense of security and strength. I could not express myself. Deprived of my mother tongue, I lost my identity and personality. I became someone different, an unidentifiable but "needy" stranger. I became a member of the "aliens" category, of a peripheral group that I had not sought and that in itself was alien to me. My life, experiences, and thoughts lost all meaning and value.

The first generation of writers who belonged to the so-called *Ausländerliteratur* predominantly dealt with issues and themes directly related to the socioeconomic conditions of life in Germany. Güney Dal, of Turkish origin, stated that his fellow countrymen's "*Konflikte mit diesem hochindustrialisierten Land, ihre Anpassungsschwierigkeiten, Entfremdung und menschliche Neigungen, ihre vielen geistigen und seelischen Auseinandersetzungen sind die thematischen Quellen meines literarischen Schaffens*" (conflicts in this highly industrialised nation, their difficulties adapting, alienation and inclinations, their numerous mental and emotional conflicts are the underlying motifs in my literary creation) (17). In his short essay *Die Fremde als der Ort der Geschichte*, Chiellino (13) recalled that "*Auslöser meiner Motivation zu schreiben war bei mir die Notwendigkeit, jene totale Isolation zu durchbrechen, die nach dem Heimatverlust in einer fremden Umgebung um mich herum entstanden war*" (the trigger for my motivation to write was the necessity to break through the total isolation that had built up around me after the loss of my home in the foreign environment).

The German-Iranian writer Said arrived in West Germany as a refugee like others who fled the aftermath of fascist dictatorships and military juntas in postwar Portugal, Spain, Greece and Turkey. Many political exiles became involved in and contributed to the culture of political and social change, and were actively engaged in the political opposition movement that strongly influenced West German society and culture in the 1960s, 1970s and 1980s. Said, who for political reasons was forced to escape from Iran during the rule of the Shah, wrote despondently about his inspiration to write: "*die Einsamkeit des Exils drängt zur Aussprache, zum Sprechen—miteinander, mit den anderen*" (the loneliness of exile urges to speak out, to communicate—together, with others) **(18)**.

Common among the writers of the so-called first generation, regardless of their personal circumstances, beliefs or political convictions, was a shared sense of homelessness, their experience of being uprooted and of their attempts in coming to terms with a new culture and language. At this first stage of a migrant literature, many authors wrote in their first language. Some, like the Turkish Germans Aras Ören or Günez Dal **(Tanzer 306)**, for example, continued to write German literature in their respective language.

ARRIVAL

At the beginning of the 1980s, Schmidt-Bergmann identified a second phase in the *Gastarbeiterliteratur*:

> Es lässt sich als ein 'Schreiben in fremder Sprache' um-schreiben. Es ist die Generation der in den fünfziger Jahren Geborenen, die sich die Frage stellt: "Wohin gehöre ich?" Damit beginnt ein Prozess, der sich nicht mehr in Polaritäten und Konfrontationen vollzieht und beginnt, die deutsche Sprache als eigene Literatursprache zu akzeptieren. (104)

> It can be described as "writing in a foreign language." It is the generation of those born in the 1950s who ask themselves: "Where do I belong?" Now a process begins that isn't mere-ly defined by polarities and confrontation anymore, but that embarks on accepting German as one's own literary language.

For these authors switching to German as their writing language on the one hand meant arrival and settling down, acknowledging the German culture as their new intellectual home. By the same token, it also represented a final border crossing: Abandoning, literally, their first language and culture, it represented doubt and demanded a to-tal reorientation in a new language. Arriving in another culture pre-cipitated assimilation and conformity, and language was easily experi-enced as an instrument of dominance and power: For many authors, the foreign language, like an adversary, had to be conquered and mas-tered. In his essay "*Der Fremde wohnt in der Sprache*," Franco Bion-di touched upon a common migrant experience when he wrote that

> Am Anfang meiner deutschsprachigen Karriere empfand ich mich in der deutschen Sprache dermaßen in Frage gestellt, dass mich eine tiefe Bessessenheit erfasste alles von der deutschen Sprache Gehörte zu beherrschen. Es zu beherrschen um nicht mehr in Frage gestellt zu werden ... ich erfuhr die

Sprache als eine fremde Macht, der ich ausgeliefert war und gegen deren Omnipotenz ich kämpfen musste. (29)

At the beginning of my writing career in German I felt questioned to such an extent that I was overcome by a strong obsession to master every aspect of the language . . . I experienced the language as a foreign power I was exposed to and whose omnipotence I had to fight against.

This position of vulnerability and impotence was further aggravated by entrenched attitudes directed at non-native German writers commonly found among representatives of the literary establishment and the publishing industry. The literary productions of the *Ausländer* were often judged purely on the basis of ethnicity, or rather the fact that these authors were non-German, and therefore measured within an elitist language system, an impermeable standard with *Hochdeutsch* (High German) as the benchmark. Whereas native German writers triggered praise and accolades for literary invention and experimentation, for deviation and difference in their writing, migrant writers, who brought into play the tensions and frictions between languages (and cultures) in their writing, found themselves patronized or rejected. Winkler-Pöhler summarized Yüksel Pazarkaya's complaint that

Man wird nur noch daran gemessen, ob man die grammatikalisch richtige Redewendung gebraucht . . . Sie legen zweierlei Maß an: Was bei bekannten deutschen Autoren als interessante Verfremdung gewertet wird, ist bei ausländischen Autoren von vornherein als nicht genügende Beherrschung der deutschen Sprache angesehen. (53)

The only assessment criteria [of publishers] is whether an author produced proper grammatical expressions, which is a double standard: an interesting estrangement in a text by a famous German author is considered a lack of competence in the German language of a foreign author.

In his short text *"Aus dem Ghetto heraus"* another author, Jusuf Naoum (79), related a corresponding episode in which the editor of a large publishing house in Germany rejected the work of a non-German writer with the explanation: *"Mit Ihren Metaphern kann ich nichts an-fangen. Wenn Sie an einer Veröffentlichung interessiert sind, dann müssen Sie sich grundsätzlich an den deutschen Geschmack anpassen"* (I don't know what to make of your metaphors. If you are interested in publishing your work you have to adapt to the German taste). Proficiency in the adopted language alone decided whether integration was accomplished or not, a measuring stick that perpetuated and reinvented the migrants' outsider status; their foreignness, the accent, oral or written, betrayed all confidence of belonging and served as an instrument of exclusion.

In *Literatur und Identität in der Fremde*, Gino Chiellino drew attention to an example of publishing practice in the early stages of migrant writing in West Germany: the aestheticizing of the so-called *Ausländerdeutsch* in standardized "foreign" literary productions. Marianne Herzog's coauthorship in the autobiographical notes of Yugoslav writer Vera Kamenko, published under the title *Unter uns war Krieg*, consisted of rewriting and editing the original text by correcting, repairing the fractured German of the original text and subjecting it to aesthetic norms and writing conventions that made the book readable. Herzog admitted in the preface that she added independence to the writing but also that she subtracted the writer's encounter with the language, her inconsistencies and frictions (*Literatur* 87). Kamenko's inconsistencies in German, the conflict with the language reflected, however, the author's fractured reality as a migrant in Germany— devoid of her broken, non-fluent German voice the text was deprived of its motive, its authenticity.

Seen in this light, the foreign language can be perceived as monolithic, immutable and sacrosanct, the standard language as a system of exclusion and the scrupulous mastery of it as an impossible ideal, a Sisyphean undertaking. But at its very core, language is not a closed system and, as Paul Celan urged in his Bremer Literatupreis address, it is not inaccessible either; in fact, it is only language that remains *"er-*

reichbar, nah und unverloren ... inmitten der Verluste" (within reach, close and present, amid all losses) (185). Language for Celan encompassed *"Sprechen, um mich zu orientieren, um zu erkunden, wo ich mich befand und wohin es mit mir wollte, um mir Wirklichkeit zu entwerfen"* (speaking to orientate myself, to find out where I was and where I was headed, to construct reality for myself) (186).

The motion of creating and locating presence and actuality is at the very centre of writing, and the different language backgrounds make "foreign" writers rather susceptible to the maelstrom of the foreign language ground, and thus its latent creative potential. In their intense exchanges with language, the foreign writers are prone to perceive the second language more acutely than monolingual native speakers who have no recourse to a contrastive perception; in fact, no perspective at all from the outside. It is this distanced, exterior view that can have an invigorating effect on writing and on language. It also has the potential to heighten the awareness of both native and non-native languages by recognizing fossilized, formulaic language standards by resisting pressures to conform to a linguistic system that appears, or presents itself as closed and inaccessible. Writing in French, for example, afforded Samuel Beckett greater simplicity and objectivity and "the freedom to concentrate on a more direct expression of the search for 'being' ... using French also enabled him to 'cut away the excess, to strip away the colour' and to concentrate more on the music of the language, its sounds and its rhythms." (Knowlson 357)

The double perspective inherent in the complementarity of two languages promotes an asserting and inhabiting of new language ground. Taking charge of language to make a stance against prescriptive conventions and clichés necessitates a claim, taking one's place. In this vein, Hein-Khatib proposed that

> ... die literarische Aneignung einer Sprache nur dann gelingt wenn man diese Sprache "verfremdet" sie in gewissem Masse ihren Konventionen "entfremdet" (was selbstverständlich deren Kenntnis voraussetzt), sie so ummodeliert bis der "persönliche" Sinn, die eigenen Vorstellungen und die spezi-

fischen, oft mit anderen Sprachen verwobenen Erfahrungen des/der Autorin in ihr zum Ausdruck gebracht werden können. (99)

... the literary appropriation of a language can only be successful if that language is "alienated," if it is to some extent "estranged" from its conventions (which of course requires a thorough knowledge of it) and shaped so that the "personal" sense, the author's own imaginations and the specific experiences often entwined with other languages can be expressed.

Libuse Monikova, who left Czechoslovakia in 1971 and settled in West Germany, where she began to write her first novel, *Die Schädigung*, in Czech, switched languages at some stage in the working process and continued to write in German from then on, although Germany or German culture was never considered home, never represented a centre, as she pointed out in an interview, and *"wenn man kein Zentrum hat, hat man auch keine Ränder"* (if someone doesn't have a centre there are no edges either) (qtd. in Braunbeck 453). But perhaps it was her fellow Bohemian Franz Kafka who provided that inspirational link:

Meiner Beschäftigung mit Kafka verdanke ich die Einsicht, daß Sprachmangel unter Umständen zur Stärke werden kann, zur Stärke des Ausdrucks, weil kein Wort selbstverständlich, in seiner Bedeutung gesichert erscheint, jedes ist neu, und die Verantwortung trägt der Autor, ich schreibe, indem ich mich in der Sprache durchtaste, manchmal an Bedeutungen heran, die bis zur Niederschrift unbewußt bleiben: diese Suche kommt ursprünglich aus der Fremdsprachlichkeit, heute weist sie mich als Autor aus. (qtd. in Alms 143)

My preoccupation with Kafka led to the realization that language deficiency can possibly turn to strength, a strength of expression, because no word is taken for granted or appears secure in its signification, each is new, and the responsibility is with the author; I write by probing my way into language, to meanings sometimes that remain subconscious until they are written down: This probing originated in foreign-language writing, today it identifies me as an author.

Inhabiting a language in this sense also provokes a different cultural view; it potentially presents itself as a liberation from the confines of the first language, it opens other vistas than those the first language alone could have afforded. The Bulgarian Tzveta Sofronieva, who writes poetry and prose in German, her fourth language, is adamant and programmatic about shaping and renewing a foreign language beyond mere linguistic features: "*Die Frage ist, wie weit wir Andersartigkeit hereinbringen können und innerhalb der deutschen Sprache bleiben können, ich meine Andersartigkeit der Bilder und Denkweisen, nicht der Grammatik*" (the question is in how far it is possible to introduce difference and remain within the German language, I mean a difference in imagery and disposition, not in grammar) (159).

I.ii.

THE FOREIGN WORD

> Gerade die Fremdheit einer Sprache aber ist es, das "Unver-
> trautsein" mit ihr, die Distanz zwischen den innersten Emp-
> findungen und den fremden Wörtern, die durch eine Sprach-
> grenzüberschreitung so offensichtlich werdende Arbitrarität
> von signifié und significant, die den Bruch mit der Norm er-
> leichtern. (Hein Kathib 100)

> But it is particularly the foreignness of a language, the "unfa-
> miliarity" with it, the distance between the inner perceptions
> and the foreign word, the obvious arbitrariness of signified and
> significant that facilitate the breach with the norm.

Writing in another language or languages and the ensuing encounters
with the foreign can harbour disorienting and challenging detours.
Ota Filip, one of the first recipients of the Chamisso Prize, wrote
about the disconcerting hybrid state of being at the fault line between
two languages and cultures—Czech and German—and the inherent
condition of uncertainty. Despite the fact that Filip has been writing
and publishing in German for decades, German remains an enigma,
and instead of reconciling a place for both languages, he has been estranged from them, they have both become foreign languages: "*Ich
lebe in einer sprachlich geteilten, oder auf eine unheimliche Art und Weise
eingekreisten Welt und bin—sprachlich betrachtet—wahrscheinlich nir-
gendwo zu Hause*" (I live in a linguistically divided, or, in an uncanny
sense encircled world, and I am—from a language point of view—
probably nowhere at home). This state of uncertainty or instability is
exacerbated by the incompatibility, the autarky both languages claim
outside of the writer's reach or control. Filip perceives his languages
under constant threat interfering with, unbalancing each other, becoming mutually exclusive:

> Wenn ich deutsch schreibe . . . überfällt mich immer öfter eine
> besonders beklemmende Art von metaphysischer Angst, dass

ich mein Tschechisch verliere, leichtsinnig aufgebe, dass ich auf eine seltsame Art und Weise sprachlich zerspringe. Und wenn ich tschechisch schreibe, zu viel tschechisch lese oder rede, fühle ich, wie aus mir mein angelerntes Deutsch entweicht, wie die Luft aus einem Ball.

When I write in German I'm evermore overcome by a particularly stifling kind of metaphysical fear that I might lose or carelessly give up my Czech, that, in a strange way or fashion, I might burst linguistically. And when I write in Czech, or read or talk too much Czech, I feel how my acquired German escapes, like the air from a balloon.

The artificial, trivial construct of language mastery as a competence achieved and forever fixed and secured is dubious: "*Mit meinen zwei Sprachen bekomme ich immer häufiger Schwierigkeiten; ich spreche sie nicht spontan, sondern auf eine seltsame Art und Weise bewusst*" (I find my two languages increasingly difficult: I don't speak them spontaneously but in a strange way consciously) (Filip). The interplay between languages only emphasizes what is also at stake in each one of them: that in creating language it has to be sought anew, over and again demarcated and reinvented, that it is not a finite accomplishment, a task completed, but that it presents the writer with a continually unstable terrain; the uncertainties and alienations only highlight the state of instability inherent in pursuing language(s), in writing. Filip's experiences show that writing in a foreign language is not a one-way street, but that it simultaneously impacts on the first language, that there are reverberations, that there is an exchange, a dialogue at work.

Yoko Tawada, who writes in Japanese and German, contemplated the act of creative extinction as a result of writing in two languages, of constantly struggling to regain a foothold when leaving one language and searching for a re-entry point into the other. The speechlessness she encounters in this process is, however, her creative point of departure, a place where set structures and meanings have temporarily been erased by the other, "previous" language. It is an aesthetic challenge to break out of language conventions and dwell in an empty vacant expanse where she is vulnerable and unsettled:

Jedes Mal, wenn ich intensiv an einem japanischen Text gearbeitet habe, kann ich keinen Text mehr in der deutschen Sprache verfassen. Mühsam krieche ich wieder in die erneut verfremdete deutsche Sprache hinein, blind und verletzbar, Schritt für Schritt taste ich Wörter ab, bis ich mich wieder im Schreiben befinde. Dann habe ich aber ein Gefühl, als hätte ich nie im Leben auf Japanisch geschrieben. Mit fällt kein japanisches Wort mehr ein, das mich zum Schreiben motivieren könnte. Alle Wörter sind tot, genauer gesagt, nicht die Wörter, sondern ich bin tot in dieser Sprache. Ich setze trotzdem japanische Schriftzeichen aufs Papier, eines nach dem anderen. Langsam fangen die Schriftzeichen an, Bilder, Wörter, Ideen hervorzurufen, um mit ihnen zu kommunizieren. Die Sprachen tun in einem solchen Moment so, als würden sie den Menschen bei einem Ausdruck helfen. Ich glaube aber nicht an den guten Willen der Sprachen. Sie sind die Monster, die am liebsten jeden "Ausdruck" zerstören wollen. Gerade diese Zerstörung habe ich bewusst als ein literarisches Verfahren gewählt. Ich will am Beginn jedes neuen Textes an den Punkt Null zurückgeworfen werden, den Punkt der Sprachlosigkeit, an dem kein Satz selbstverständlich einen Sinn produzieren kann. Mich zieht am meisten die Literatur an, die diese Ohnmacht der Sprachlosigkeit kennt. (qtd. in Gutjahr 22)

Each time after having worked intensely on a Japanese text, I'm unable to write anything in German. Arduously I crawl back into an estranged German again, blind and vulnerable, step-by-step I sound out words until I find myself writing again. But then I have a feeling as if I have never before written in Japanese. I can't think of any Japanese word that could motivate me to write. All the words are dead, or more precisely, not the words, but I am dead in that language. Nevertheless, I put Japanese characters on paper, one after the other. Slowly the characters conjure up images, words, ideas in order to communicate with them. In such a moment, the languages pretend to be helping people with an expression. But I don't believe in the goodwill of languages. They are monsters that would like to destroy every possible expression. I have chosen this destruction deliberately as a literary process. I want to be thrown back to the beginning, to the point of speechlessness where no sentence can naturally produce meaning. I am most drawn to literature that is aware of the impotence of speechlessness.

Franco Biondi (30) explored the metaphor of foreignness in *"Die Fremde wohnt in der Sprache"* and remarked that *"in der deutschen Sprache habe ich mir ein Zuhause eingerichtet. Dennoch bleibt in der Sprache die Fremde wohnen. Sprache ist an und für sich Fremde. Jeder Mensch muss in seinem Leben sein eigenes Zuhause in der Sprache errichten. Ein Leben lang muß er daran arbeiten, muß er die darin enthaltende Fremde bewohnbar machen"* (I've established my home in the German language. Still, the foreignness in the language remains. Language is in itself foreign. Every person has to build his own home in his language. He has to work at it all his life, has to make the foreignness inside inhabitable). The inherent foreignness of language for Biondi situates the writer in an unfamiliar context where the subjective dimension of language impacts with its "objective" counterpart. This collision promotes transition; it forces the writer to prowl deeper in the raw material of language, to calibrate word and text, to probe its tentative manifestations. *"Erzählen,"* in the words of the Austrian writer Peter Handke, *"ist eine Offenbarung"* (narrating is a revelation). Language, in a sense, constitutes a foreign object for every writer and the distance between language and its aesthetic application, its realization, is a hallmark, an indispensible part of innovative, non-formulaic writing. According to Geiser (62) *"die dichterische Verwendung von Sprache löst einen ästhetischen Verwandlungsprozess aus, der eine Art Rückübersetzung erforderlich macht auch wenn Autor und Leser dieselbe Sprache beherrschen"* (a poetic or literary use of language triggers an aesthetic transformation that requires some form of back-translation, even if the author and the reader use the same language).

The retraced word

The dramatic shift in Europe's political landscape after 1989 and the subsequent disintegration of the East, and the official disappearance, at least, of the East-West divide, saw a massive flux of emigrants from Eastern to Western European countries. This exodus also precipitated the transfer of literatures and cultures and gave way to the intercultural multiplicity of authors who became part of a new generation of writers with a non-German background. For these decidedly European authors of a new German literature, questions of identity politics became somewhat awkward and redundant as their voice and place was situated self-assuredly at equal distance between home and abroad, between now and then.

Tzveta Sofronieva dismissed the idea of a fixed exclusive belonging to a place as an infringement of her multicultural pleasure principle:

> Den Speicher der Lebenslust in mir—in der Kindheit aufgefüllt und immer wieder hier und da neu getankt—nenne ich Heimat. Heimatlosigkeit als bewußtes Verzichten auf Geborgenheit oder angebliches Verzichten auf eigenes Revier ist mir fremd. Sich zu entscheiden, jemand oder etwas nicht zu sein, gelingt nur, wenn man es schon war oder beinahe war. Gleichzeitig aber scheint mir die Mühe, unbedingt irgendwo allein zuzugehören, Zeitverschwendung und Identitätsverlust, Beschränkung der Lebenslust. Was nennen wir denn Identität? (10)

> The reservoir of my zest for life—charged in my childhood and fuelled again here and there—is what I call *Heimat*. Being without home as a deliberate refusal of emotional security or the apparent denial of one's own terrain is alien to me. Deciding not to be someone or something can only be achieved if one has been or almost has been someone before. At the same time, going through the trouble of having to belong somewhere in particular seems to me a waste of time and a loss of identity, a limitation of the zest for life. What is identity anyhow?

With the shift in the political and cultural topography, the orientation of literature, the role of language also shifted. The early manifestations of migrant literature in West Germany engaged in documenting and narrating experiences related to the trials and tribulations in a foreign land and culture, a perspective informed by the loss of place and identity. For the new generation, the self-conscious commemorations of their predecessors became ignominious, their own background a source of confidence they embraced as a chance, as their proud potential in an increasingly multi-ethnic reality. Jamal Tuschick in the sardonic, condescending jargon of the literary *Grenzgänger*, "border crosser," noted that

> Hier ist nun alles Überschuß und Chance was einmal Zweifel und Verlust war. Das Glück der späten Geburt erspart den Begünstigten nicht zuletzt die intellektuellen Krämpfe ihrer Vorgänger aus der Migrantenautoren-Generation, die ihre Publikationszusammenhänge noch in einer auf Lebenshilfe ausgerichteten "Ausländerkultur" suchen mussten, Das war eine Szene, in der Sozialarbeiter den Ton angaben. (284)

> Everything that used to be doubt and loss now is exuberance and opportunity. The benefactors of the second generation are spared the intellectual distortions of their predecessors belonging to the migrant author generation, which had to find its publication contexts within a welfare-oriented *"Ausländerkultur."* It was a culture where social workers called the shots.

For the older generation of migrant writers, the use of language, as Andre Aciman in his introduction to *Letters of Transit* so poignantly explored, is often bound up with a resistance on the part of the émigré writer to adapt, "to let go of things that are at once private and timeless, the way childhood and ritual and memory are private and timeless" (11). The new generation doesn't move across borders with the weighty cultural and political baggage of the older migrants, and its writing shows no patina of nostalgia either. Marica Bodrožić, who left her Croatian homeland as a young girl, takes a curious and, in a sense, untainted look at the interrelationship between first and second language. The interaction between languages is not invested with loss and yearning but rather with finding and retrieving: "*Die Doppelbödige der ersten Sprache*," she writes in her lyrical essay collection *Sterne erben, Sterne färben*, "*es zeigte sich erst beim Bestehen in der zweiten*" (the ambiguity of the first language only revealed itself in accomplishing the second) (95). She remembers becoming aware of arriving in herself in German, her second language:

> Viele Jahre nach dem Ausfall der Stimme schrieb ich an meinem ersten Buch. Die deutsche Sprache führte mich zielgenau an alle Lücken des ersten Lebens heran. Menschengesichter, der Geruch des Fenchels, die Flut der Bilder und Farben, alles stand da in den deutschen Wörtern, als sei es dort schon immer gewesen, als habe die deutsche Sprache stets einen Abgesandten, einen Mitbewohner in mir getragen, geboren geradezu, und dann machte sie mich mittels dieses Helfers zu einem Menschen mit Erinnerung. Jedes Wort trägt ein eigenes Schwingungsfeld von Bewußtsein in sich. Um so rätselhafter für mich selbst, mich an das Ersterlebte in der deutschen Sprache zu erinnern. (101)

> Many years after the loss of my voice I wrote my first book. German led me unerringly to all the blanks of my first life. Human faces, the smell of fennel, the flood of images and colours, all of it was written in German words, as if it had always been there, as if the German language had always been carrying, giving birth, almost, to an envoy, a co-inhabitant within me; and then, with the help of this assistant, I became a person with a memory. Each word carries a particular oscillating field of consciousness within itself. All the more mysterious for myself to remember my very first experiences in the German language.

The second language enabled Bodrožić to envision, to name the imagery of the first; it was only through writing that both languages could be reconciled, brought together. She also questioned whether her first language wasn't something altogether hybrid, something entirely imperfect, a mixture consisting of language crossings and inklings of different dialects (96). The childhood memories imprinted in her first language are fathomed, sounded out in German:

> Die Selbstverständlichkeit, mit der die Wälder des Slawischen in mir liegen, wird mir erst im *Schreibengehen* bewußt. Dieses Unterpfand, das immer aus der ersten Sprache herauftönt und mich endlich zu jemand macht, der etwas von sich sagen kann. Aber erst in der deutschen Sprache wird mein eigenes Zuhause für mich selbst hörbar. (11)

> Only in the act of writing have I become aware of the naturalness in which the thickets of the Slavic language reside within me, the pledge that always resonates from the first language and that has made me become someone who can say something about herself. But only in German has being at home become audible to me.

Another representative of the third generation, Feridun Zaimoglou's writing career erupted rigorously with his *Kanak Sprak* texts in the 1990s. Generated by the patois of the *Kanakster*, these texts at long last gave a voice to those Germans of a Turkish background who did not fit into Germany's *Multikultur*, who renounced the ever-louder and growing demands in German society and politics for assimilation, for submission. They expressed themselves in a self-respecting and self-assured, if somewhat shrill and encoded Creole, a mix of German, Turkish infused with gesticulations and intonations borrowed from American rap and the pathos of a "good and evil" mystique. In sharp contrast to Bodrožić's sensitive, ethereal observations and reflections on the friction between language and homecoming, of finding a voice, Zaimoglu composed fast, rhythmic invectives based on recorded interviews with urban Turkish fringe dwellers of the second or third generation. He modified and arranged these plastic, fugitive hybrid tongues into so-called *Protokolle*, or protocols. *Kanak Sprak* derives from the derogatory term *Kanake* (wog, nigger), but here it is worn self-consciously, reflecting a proud hybrid identity; there are patent references to postcolonial struggles, to oppression and resistance, a coveted kinship with the black American urban ghetto.

> Die Wortgewalt des Kanaken drückt sich aus in einem heraus-gepreßten, kurzatmigen und hybriden Gestammel ohne Punkt und Komma, mit willkürlich gesetzten Pausen und improvisi-erten Wendungen. Der Kanake spricht seine Muttersprache nur fehlerhaft, auch das "Alemanisch" ist ihm nur bedingt geläufig. Sein Sprachschatz setzt sich aus "verkauderwelschten" Vokabeln und Redewendungen zusammen, die so in keiner der beiden Sprachen vorkommen. (13)

> The magniloquence of the *Kanak* is expressed in a compressed, short-winded and hybrid ramble without full stop and com-ma, with arbitrarily placed pauses and improvised turns. The *Kanak* is deficient in his mother tongue, and he is only part-ly familiar with German. His vocabulary consists of a hotch-potch of words and turns of phrase that don't exist in either of his languages.

The hypocrisies of *Multikultur* in Germany these young Germans en-countered and the entrenched discrimination of migrant communi-ties are the motor of their personal disenchantments and outbursts, settling scores with thirty years of German denigration and paternal-ism. Zaimoglu's attempts in resurrecting, establishing a voice and aura for the oppressed and dispossessed (rappers, addicts, poets and others abounding with subcultural shrewdness) are—ironically—reminis-cent of the "*exotischer Zauber*" (exotic charm) and "*schlampige Nostal-gie*" (sloppy nostalgia) he ascribes to the "*Müllkutscherprosa*" (garbage collector prose) of his predecessors (12). The flawed authenticity he detects in the *Ausländerliteratur* of the first generation also has to be purged from the raw, unedited speeches he assembled for the *Kanak Sprak* volume. He refers to his *Mißtöne vom Rande der Gesellschaft*, discords from the fringe, rather nonchalantly as adaptations, which gain integrity only in the creative modulations, in the "translations" of the author (Skiba 196).

Although it appears that Zaimoglu's references to his *Kanak Sprak* texts as translations are random, this method of rewriting and reconstructing original text material has had a decisive influence on the concept of translation in general; in fact, the implications of adapting a source text as a raw model for transposition into another language has determined the earliest manifestations of a translation theory in the West. Another defining issue raised incidentally by Zaimoglu's "translations" is a preliminary premise of the inner workings of translation, its imperative. The "translated" *Protokolle* exemplify a complete immersion into the jargon, the fixed phraseology of a self-contained, self-referential language milieu. They are locked in an exclusive code that is almost inaccessible to the mainstream outsider, steeped so deeply and exclusively in its mechanics that it repudiates, resists the possibility of a reopening to another language, of recovering its design in "another" translation. In a translation of the "translation" of these texts, the exchange between languages comes to a halt, the text in this regard is closed, obstructed. In "*Die Aufgabe des Übersetzers*," Walter Benjamin acknowledged this incongruity when he suggested that

> das Verhältnis des Gehalts zur Sprache [ist] völlig verschieden in Orginal und Übersetzung. Bilden nämlich diese im ersten eine gewisse Einheit . . . so bedeutet die Sprache der Übersetzung eine höhere Sprache als sie ist und bleibt dadurch ihrem eigenen Gehalt gegenüber unangemessen, gewaltig und fremd . . . *Übersetzung verpflanzt* also das Orginal in einen . . . entgültigeren Sprachbereich . . . **(15)**

> The relationship between content and language is quite different in the original and the translation. While content and language form a certain unity in the original . . . the language of the translation . . . signifies a more exalted language than its own and thus remains unsuited to its content, overpowering and alien . . . translation, ironically, transplants the original into a more definite linguistic realm . . . (*Illuminations* 76)

EDUARD STOKLOSINSKI /34

The complementarity of languages, the dialogic nature of writing, appears to be, in regard to a text's translatability, an essential prerequisite. The rearticulation of the foreign underlies a meaningful interchange in translating, the mitigation of the other, translating language. A central aspect of literary translation hinges on affecting the foreign in the original, its retrieval—the frictions and fissures, the labour of the original text, ought to remain apparent, transparent. Inadvertently, both authors sketched here, as well as the other texts represented in the anthology, carry out in their own distinct ways the charge with which Friedrich Schleiermacher entrusted translation at the beginning of the German Romantic era: to take the reader abroad for an experience of the foreign. The texts assembled in this anthology perform this mission in a quasi-circular motion, by taking the reader home, coincidently (de)solving and pre-empting the polarity, the construed antagonism between literal retrieval and fluent rewriting that has dominated translation theory from its beginnings.

THE EXPERIENCE OF THE FOREIGN IN TRANSLATION

> Labor on the letter in translation is more originary than resti-
> tution of meaning. It is through this labor that translation, on
> the one hand, restores the particular signifying process of
> works (which is more than their meaning) and, on the other
> hand, transforms the translating language. Translation stimu-
> lated the fashioning and refashioning of the great western lan-
> guages only because it labored on the letter and profoundly
> modified the translating language. As a simple restitution of
> meaning, translation could never have played this formative
> role.
>
> —Antoine Berman (297)

Fluency strategies have been predominant in the history of literary
translation in Europe from the time Cicero (106–43 BC) formulated
the first maxims he applied in his translations from the Greek, claim-
ing to have "*nec converti ut interpres, sed ut orator, sententiis isdem et
earum formis tanquam figuris, verbis ad nostram consuetudinem aptis. In
quibus non verbum pro verbo necesse habui reddere, sed genus omne ver-
borum vimque servavi*" (365) (". . . not translated them as an interpret-
er, but as an orator, keeping the same ideas and the forms, or as one
might say, the 'figures' of thought, but in language which conforms
to our usage. And in so doing, I did not hold it necessary to render
word for word, but I preserved the general style and force of the language"; Hubell 366).

Most of Cicero's prominent, albeit brief, remarks on translation
can be found in a short essay on the art of oratory, entitled "*De Optimo Genere Oratorum.*" In the text, he established that different genres
of written poetry have a distinctive, individual form and tone, while
skillful oratory requires different styles to coincide: "Sunt enim do-
cendi acutae, delectandi quasi argutae, commovendi graves" (Cicero,
356) ("for exposition and explanation they should be pointed, for en-
tertainment, bright and witty, for rousing the emotions, weighty and
impressive"; Hubell 357). The most accomplished style in oratory has

been attained by the Attic orators, among whom Demosthenes and Aeschines were the most eloquent: "*hunc si qui imitetur, eum et Attice dicturum et optime* . . ." (365) ("One who imitates him will speak in the Attic manner and in the best manner"; Hubell, 366). To elucidate the nature of Greek oratory, Cicero translated two speeches by these authors, keeping to the Roman idiom with the expressed aim of establishing a model for the Latin language "*regula, ad quam eorum dirigantur orationes qui Attice volent dicere*" (372) ("there will be a norm by which to measure the speeches of those who may wish to speak in the Attic manner"; Hubell 373).

The word-for-word metaphor and its sense-for-sense counterpart have been, exhaustingly, at the centre of writing on translation, and although a plethora of attributes, from the literal versus the fluent to the faithful and the free, have been attached to them, the *verbum pro verbo* maxim and what exactly it encompassed have in actual fact remained elusive. Olser (54) wryly pointed out that translators in antiquity "probably would have had their heads chopped off if they had come up with a string of words in the word order of the SL [source language]. I suspect on the contrary, though I have no evidence at all that they would have translated rather loosely and imprecisely, almost too much '*ad sensum.*'" A thread of evidence might be found in light of the impact the Hellenistic culture had on the formation of Latin, as well as, in late Roman antiquity, the Bible as the authoritative power in delineating the role of translation.

APPROPRIATION AND RESTORATION

In "*De optimo*," Cicero identified the proclaimed target audience for his translation project: "*putavi mihi suscipiendum laborem utilem studiosis, mihi quidem ipsi non necessarrium*" (365) ("I thought it my duty to undertake a task which will be useful to students, though not necessary for myself"; Hubell 366). In Cicero's times, rhetoric represented the highest educational echelon, the study of the art of oratory. It was taught to students who had completed the previous stage, the school of the less prestigious *grammaticus*, where pupils were instructed in "*scientia (or ars) recte loquendi*, correct speaking and reading, and *enarratio poetarum*, study of the poets" (Copeland, *Rhetoric* 12). It is important to note that a bilingual education in Latin and Greek did not exist before the reign of Augustus (27 AD), some years after Cicero's death, and that in Cicero's times the language of instruction for students of Latin rhetoric, who studied the art of oratory, was Greek, which "with its wealth of literature in prose and verse and its tradition of scientific criticism, was the inevitable language for use in schools" (Gwynn 94).

It appears that Cicero had in mind a critique and renewal of the entrenched methods of teaching, reading and exposition, the textual commentary on form and matter. According to Copeland (*Rhetoric* 9), his allusion to "literalness" was to emphasize the difference between grammar, under which translation as textual commentary was relegated, and the translation of oratory "not with the express aim to define the practice of translation itself, but rather as a way of defining the status of rhetoric in relation to grammar." In fact, literary translation did not carry much currency or prestige in the time of the Late Republic. It featured to a limited extent as a pedagogical tool in literary commentary and exercises in rhetoric, but the domestic readership had no need for translations from the Greek, as "educated Romans could just as well have gone on reading Greek literature and philosophy in the original, since they were bilingual anyway" (Lefevere 15). Literate Romans, a minute, elite minority, were able to compare and read the translated version vis-à-vis the original. Accordingly, Cicero's objective, instead of translating the original speeches, was to adapt, to assimilate them, or as Hermans pointed out, "he was intent not on reproducing in Latin what the Greek orators actually said, but on creating a Latin model of the Attic style of oratory which will be able to displace the Greek sources" (22). Following the demand to render the content and form of the source text as long as it was compatible and not conflicting with the translating language, his interpretation of the Greek text was aimed at forming, enriching, and refining Latin and also, at enhancing the prestige of the translator as an original and scholarly writer.

Just as Livius Andronicus, the first Roman poet and Greek slave who translated Homer's Odyssey into Latin, had sought to introduce the Greek epic as a vantage point from which teaching Latin literature would become possible (Marrou 251), Cicero's intention was to create a Latin model that could equal or vie with and challenge the admired ideal of Greek poetry and philosophy. In the role of rhetorician-translator, Cicero endeavored to enhance a linguistically deficient Latin by advancing its status to a language of aesthetic and philosophical inquiry. To this end, the original Greek texts had to be resignified, the source text appropriated, adapted, reinvented.

> For Roman translators, the task of transferring a text from language to language could be perceived as an exercise in comparative stylistics, since they were freed from the exigencies of having to "make known" either the form or the content *per se*, and consequently did not need to subordinate themselves to the frame of the original. The good translator, therefore, presupposed the reader's acquaintance with the SL text and was bound by that knowledge, for any assessment of his skill as translator would be based on the creative use he was able to make of his model. (Bassnett-McGuirre 45)

Over the succeeding centuries, Latin replaced Greek as the dominant language in the Roman Empire. In a linguistic environment substantially different from that of Cicero's times, the demand for translations increased, "but they were no longer literary exercises as they had been in the golden age; they were intended for publication, to supply the

Latin public with a foreign literature that they could no longer read in the original" (Marrou 262); consequently, translations grew in status. Christianity had consolidated itself as a religious and political power, reinforced by the institution of the Roman Catholic Church and the Bible as the central dogmatic canon. With it, the focus of philosophical and aesthetic inquiry shifted, also resetting the parameters for the objectives of translation. The source text, which had functioned as a mere model or point of departure in the expansion of Latin as a language of scholarly inquiry, now embodied authority and ideological significance in the form of the Scriptures. Christian theology regarded as paramount the divine, extra-linguistic truth of the sacred text, which had to be guarded against fallible interpretation and misreading. Copeland proposed that "patristic translation theory was concerned mainly with recuperating the signified," i.e., with the recovery of the original:

> Whereas Roman theory seeks to erase difference by foreclosing the originary claims of the source and substituting Latin for Greek, patristic criticism seeks more to resolve difference by pointing toward a communality of source and target in terms of the immanence of meaning. (*Fortunes*, 20)

These ideological changes also affected the status of translations and led to a shift in its design and purpose. Hieronymus (the later St Jerome) translated the Bible into what became known as the Vulgate, the first Latin version of the text, a task that involved consultation and revision of older Latin texts and translations from the Greek Septuagint as well as Hebrew texts. He formulated his ideas on translation in an epistle to Pammachius entitled "*De optimo genere interpretandi*," written in 395 AD, and as the title suggests, in close proximity to Cicero's treatise with one notable exception:

> Ego enim non solum fateor, sed libera voce profiteor, me in interpretatione Graecorú, absque scripturis sanctis, ubi & verborum ordo & mysterium est, nó verbum è verbo, sed sensum exprimere de sensu. (Hieronymi 366)

> I not only admit, but freely proclaim that in translation from
> the Greek—except in the case of Sacred Scriptures where the
> very order of the words is a mystery—I render not word for
> word, but sense for sense. (Jerome 23)

Hieronymus was not advocating a word-for-word approach for translation. On the contrary, in reference to Cicero and Horace, he used
the idea of "*verbum e verbo*" as a demarcation, pointing out "the arti-
ficiality of the literal method" (Pratt 3) which is invested with negative
connotations: "If I translate word by word, it sounds absurd" and "the
syntax becomes ridiculous, and the most eloquent poet barely articulate" (Jerome 24). However, in a slight but crucial point of departure
from the Ciceronian model, the translator conceded, if only in the
case of the Scriptures, the formal composition of a text to be integral
to its meaning, inscribing an extralingual "truth" beyond the reach of
interpretation. If the word weighs heavier than its implied meaning,
if the original text can not be embellished with interpretative force because of its ideological (or cultural) gravity, it has to be restored in its
original signification, an artefact reconstituted with the primacy of the
word over sense and structure over style. Whether or not Jerome's letter to Pammachius has to be read as a tactical defence to counter-accu-
sations of deliberate mistranslations made against him as Hermans (20)
has suggested, Jerome's statement institutes a first recognition of the
original's integrity in translation.

With the Buber-Rosenzweig Bible translation at the beginning of
the twentieth century, this fragmentary premise found its most radi-
cal realization in the retrieval, the uncovering of the Hebrew in the
German tongue, the attempt at making the other language, the original, present, audible: "To get down to the basic meaning of each word
was the uppermost principle, to lay bare the meaning of the words
in their utter concreteness, to strip them of the abstract—theologi-
cal or philosophical—accretions that had made them intangible and
shrouded them in terms and notions" (Reichert 178) as a reverberation
of the truth.

Over the centuries following Hieronymus, however, the fluency
maxim continued to be applied in the praxis of translation. A pre-

liminary notion about the integrity of the original lay dormant in its
ideological sanctuary, and not until the beginning of the nineteenth
century did these rudimentary reflections on translation in classical
antiquity undergo a systematic, secularized reworking.

READABILITY AND ESTRANGEMENT

By the time Alexander Tytler wrote his *Essay on the Principles of Translation* in 1791, sense for sense or fluency tradition had been well and truly established in Europe. Translations in the fashion of the French *belle infidels*, for example, aspired to improve upon and adorn the original by transplanting the foreign author firmly into French soil, by presenting *Aeneas* in the cloak of a "cavalier français" (Stackelberg 20). In Tytler's treatise, the first systematic approach to literary translation, he proposed three general laws that constituted "good" translation, underpinned by copious examples from poetry and prose and instances of successes and failures regarding his maxims:

   I. That the translation should give a complete transcript of the ideas of the original work.
   II. That the style and manner of writing should be of the same character with that of the original.
   III. That the translation should have all the ease of original composition. (15)

In the application of the first law, the translator was required to use her/his discretion to improve the text, to intervene where style and consonance are lacking or obstructed: "A liberty which a translator may take," is to correct "what appears to him a careless or inaccurate expression of the original" (Tytler 59), and to "add to the idea of the original what may appear to give greater force or illustration" (Tytler 38). Furthermore, it was the translator's duty to rise above and rewrite what s/he perceives as flaws in the original, since "to imitate the obscurity or ambiguity of the original is a fault" (31). The failure to abide by the style and manner of the original, its character, will lead to unedifying, undesired results: "the grave style of the original becomes heavy and formal in the translation; the elevated swells into bombast, the lively froths up into the petulant, and the simple and *naif* degenerates into the childish and insipid" (133). In order to master the third law, the translator must "adopt the very soul of his author, which must speak through his own organs" (203), the ease of the original requiring the most correct taste "to prevent that ease from degenerating into licentiousness" (210).

Tytler's prescriptive approach in his thoughts on translation was entirely immersed, "transfused" (159) as it were, in the target language; all possible dialogue or interchange between languages—their reciprocal impact—is cancelled. The translator's task is to assimilate the text to the taste of the literary canon, to assess its merits and faults and, decisively and liberally, to edit the original, that is, "amplify and retrench" where in her/his judgement it needs refinement. Tytler's objective is a complete subsumption of the original into the target culture: "A translator ought always to figure to himself, in what manner the original author would have expressed himself, if he had written in the language of the translation" (Tytler 189).

Tytler's norms can be read as the contemporary antithesis to the German translation project of the early nineteenth century: While the former is the attempt at an empirical prescription of translation principles, the latter is of a more critical, speculative nature, a historical, philosophical inquiry into the scope of translation. Schleiermacher, as its most methodical proponent, suggested that not only is it unattainable to demand that the author speak as if s/he would have written in the translating language, but that this notion is irreconcilabile with the charge of translation.

In his seminal lecture *Über die verschiedenen Methoden des Übersetzens* from 1813, Schleiermacher begins his enquiry by distinguishing *dolmetschen*, interpreting, and translation. Here, in reversal of the Ciceronian model, translation is reserved for the arts and philosophy and it only pertains to works where the substance of the text is determined by the distinctive imprint of the author, where it coincides and merges uniquely with the spirit of the language on which it is built and conditioned (Schleiermacher 41). If the creative force of a language is bound to the particular characteristics of a culture, then everyone's knowledge and the ability to use and express it is mainly and distinctly formed in and through that language. Given the singular quality of literature and philosophy, no signification in one language captures the same diversity of relationships in the other (42). Seen in this light, translation, he suggests, seems like an impossible, foolish undertaking. Indeed, the two common methods devised to acquaint the reader with the foreign work are contrary to the task of translation: The paraphrase attempts to conquer the irrationality of language, to capture details of the original by elucidating or reducing it and thus manages to reproduce some of the content but nothing of the impression the original text imparts (45). The *Nachbildung*, the afterimage, on the other hand, bows to the irrationality of language and attempts to construct a coherent whole from parts that are markedly different from the original—it aims to reproduce its effect by foresaking the work's identity. Discarding both, Schleiermacher concludes that, essentially, there are only two incompatible propositions possible in translation: Either the translator moves the reader toward the author or he moves the author toward the reader (47), and only the former motion, although porous and fraught with difficulty, is relevant and essential to the implications of translation.

Schleiermacher then proposes to move reader and author together by shifting the focus from the reader to the original text as the critical vantage point. Reader and author must meet at a certain point, and that point will always be the translator, carrying out the inherent charge of translation: that the reader perceives the spirit of a foreign language and the spirit of a foreign writer. In order to enable this experience of the foreign, two general conditions have to be met: An encounter with the foreign is appreciated and embraced by the translating culture as a whole so as to promote and cultivate a receptive climate for foreign literatures, and the translating language has to be endowed with a certain capacity to be bent toward, to be affected by, the translated language (58).

About a century later, Walter Benjamin contemplated this signifying process in the introduction to his translation of Baudelaire's *Tableaux Parisiens*. In regard to the reader, Benjamin contended, a literary work of art says very little to those who understand it; it is, in fact, not meant for the reader, and if the original is not meant for the reader, how can a translation be assigned that role? The essence of a work of art is not communication, and a translation that aims to convey information conveys nothing but the inessential, the characteris-

tic of a bad translation (Benjamin, *Illuminations* 9). The essence it is assumed, or what might be termed "the poetic, the unfathomable, etc.,"
can only be brought across if the translator is a poet herself. Benjamin
concludes, however, that this is simply another characteristic of bad
translation, as it tends to represent the inaccurate transfer of an inessential content (Benjamin, *Illuminations* 9).

Benjamin's essay has become a seminal text in contemporary translation studies and has released a plethora of discussions and commen-
taries, not least among scholars with a deconstructionist bent. One of
these readings is Carol Jacob's "The Monstrosity of Translation," an
engaging excursion through Benjamin's "translation of translation" (Jacobs 76) where, she argues, definitions are dislocated, words are directed against their conventional meaning, their familiarities estranged,
dodging comprehension (79). However, in comparing the original
with the widely published English translation of Henry Zohn, she
detects an attempt to balance and redress the original's foreignness, a
tendency that contravenes the essential quality Benjamin ascribes to
his translation.

> Wie nämlich Scherben eines Gefäßes, um sich zusammenfü-
> gen zu lassen, in den kleinsten Einzelheiten einander zu fol-
> gen, doch nicht so zu gleichen haben, so muss, anstatt dem
> Sinn . . . (Benjamin 79)

> Fragments of a vessel which are to be glued together must
> match one another in the smallest details, although they need
> not be like one another . . . (Benjamin, *Illuminations* 18)

The main feature of Zohn's translation is its underlying rationale to
clarify, to absorb the original into an apparently coherent context. But
in the attempt to achieve fluency in the translation and in rendering
the text readable for an American academic audience, it becomes im-
precise, flawed, suggesting something else, something different than
the original. Carol Jacobs translated the same segment in the following manner:

> Just as fragments of a vessel, in order to be articulated togeth-
> er, must follow one another in the smallest detail but need not
> resemble one another . . . (84)

Jacobs comments on her version that "in the literal translation above,
the passage leaves things incomplete. With the joining together of
translation and original, language remains a broken part" (84). Whereas Zohn attempts to "repair" the vessel by gluing the broken pieces together in an attempt to create coherence and unity, Jacobs articulates
the pieces, like scattered pieces of an archaeological find, fitting them
together without the need for a final form. Zohn translates the original *einander zu folgen* as "match one another"; in contrast, Jacobs's
version retains the closer, more exacting suggestion of this phrase—
"follow one another." In Jacob's version, as in Zohn's, however, the
translated excerpts imply an intention, introduce a modality that is
not present in the original; both writers translate "must follow" or
"must match," respectively. In Benjamin's text, two infinitive clauses
simply follow one another, and in the translated passages above this
"fragmentary" mode of syntax is not articulated. Here is another version of the same passage, following closely the author's mode of intention:

> Just as shards of a vessel in order to be fitted together, to follow
> one another in the smallest detail, do not have to resemble one
> another . . .

It is in this part of the essay where Benjamin explores the scope of
Wörtlichkeit—literalness. The sense of the word in the original cannot be reproduced in the translation, "for sense in its poetic significance is not limited to meaning, but derives from the connotations
conveyed by the word chosen to express it" (Benjamin 78). The translation is, therefore, to refrain from resembling the meaning of the original and instead ought to attempt to form in the translating language
the original's mode of meaning, "follow one another" to use Jacobs's
translation as a metaphor, particularly in regard to literary works: The
foreign textuality has to be uncovered in detail and with care. Zohn's

translation presents the original text more fluently and cohesively than it is, and in doing so, Zorn also obscures and renders it immaterial. His approach removes the text from the author's mode of meaning, which here is inconclusive, elusive.

The translation of writing with a distinct, innovative texture necessitates a reconsidering of the weight of the foreign word and form. An apt approach to the translation of unique literary prose depends on the recovery, the restoration of its origin, its authenticity, the "thorough" rendering of the text's inconclusiveness—to that effect the translation needs to be guided by the original. Although writing with "foreign" imprints is intrinsically aberrant, perceptions persist that "carrying over" deviant, estranging features of the foreign into the translating language constitutes negative, inappropriate intrusions. Implications of this tendency to obscure, to reduce and to simplify the underlying relationship and interaction between the translating and translated language are that the aesthetics of the original text are at best diminished, at worse erased. A translation that attempts to conclude the original essentially brings about its extinction.

III.

Translators at Work

This section will take a closer look at the praxis of current translation strategies and tendencies and their impact on the original and translating language by examining published English translations of two authors present in this anthology. Some of the German Japanese writer Yoko Tawada's earlier prose texts and literary essays have been published in English and have appeared in a short-story collection entitled *Where Europe Begins* in 2002, translated by Susan Bernofsky. The novels by Herta Müller have been translated into English. Perhaps her best known work in translation is *Herztier*, which won the Impac Dublin Literary Award in an English version by Michael Hofmann titled *The Land of the Green Plums*, originally published by Metropolitan Books in 1996. Both translators are renowned practitioners in their field who have translated prominent authors of German literature. Bernofsky, for example, distinguished herself with her recent reintroduction of Robert Walser, the Swiss writer and poet, to an Anglophone readership; Hofmann, a poet in his own right, has an impressive track record of translations, including novels by Thomas Bernhard, Joseph Roth, and Franz Kafka.

In the following passages of translation, the opening paragraphs of each translated text are discussed with reference to the French translation theorist Antoine Berman's brief "analytic of translation," a tentative framework that has identified various textual deformation tendencies commonly at work in translating and editing foreign prose **(Berman 288)**. Among the more pervasive tendencies he emphasises rationalization, for instance, as a strategy that aims to establish order by recomposing punctuation, syntax and word classes, with the result of stifling textual abundance. Other editorial devices include clarification, which, according to Berman, renders the opaque transparent by interpreting tentative meanings, and expansion, a tendency to inflate, to stretch and consequently thin out the translating language, to "flatten ... what is essentially deep" **(290)**. Ennoblement, Berman defines as a rewriting exercise for elegance and readability in the classic tradition: by removing clumsiness and clutter the original's prosaic elegance is enhanced, but by pruning imperfections "the depth, the strata, the polylogism of language" (Berman 289) are obscured or erased, the text becomes abstract. A brief comparison of original and translation in the following paragraphs aims to contextualise Berman's analysis.

III.i.

SUSAN BERNOFSKY'S TRANSLATION
OF YOKO TAWADA'S *ZUNGENTANZ*

Where Europe Begins contains a short story entitled "Tongue Dance," translated by Susan Bernofsky. It was originally published in German as *"Zungentanz"* in Tawada's short-story collection *Ueberseezungen* (2002), the same book from which the three stories of this anthology were taken. The opening paragraph in *"Zungentanz"* reads:

> Wenn ich aufwache, ist meine Zunge immer etwas geschwollen und viel zu groß, um sich in der Mundhöhle bewegen zu können. Sie versperrt mir den Atemweg, ich spüre einen Druck auf die Lungen. Wie lange noch dieses Ersticken? frage ich mich, und schon schrumpft sie. Meine Zunge erinnert mich dann an einen verbrauchten Schwamm, steif und trocken zieht sie sich langsam in die Speiseröhre zurück, dabei nimmt sie meinen ganzen Kopf mit. (9)

In Susan Bernofsky's English translation, the paragraph has been rendered as follows:

> My tongue is always somewhat swollen when I wake up, much too large to move easily within my mouth. It blocks my windpipe, I can feel the pressure building up in my lungs. How much longer do I have to suffocate? I wonder, and at once it begins to shrink. At such moments my tongue reminds me of a worn-out sponge: dry and stiff, it retreats into my esophagus, dragging the rest of my head behind it. (115)

The passage reads fluidly and smoothly due to several translatorial arrangements that have standardized Tawada's original text. In the first sentence, for instance, the translator has amended and restyled five different textual elements. First, the syntax has been changed by moving the dependent clause *wenn ich aufwache* (when I wake up) from its initial position to the end of the first clause, after which the original's conjunction *und* has been deleted. *Mundhöhle*, a compound noun (literally "mouth cave"), has been reduced or simplified to the more general English description "mouth" and also subjected to the possessive pronoun "my," whereas the original *Mundhöhle* features only a definite article, *die*. Finally, in the English version, the tongue can't move "easily"—the adverb "easily" has been introduced—while in the German original the tongue simply can't move and the verb remains without the qualification of an adverb.

As indicated in the first chapter, Tawada's prose probing is very curious and exacting in regard to words and their semantic fixtures; she is intrigued by their "looks" and onomatopoetic allusions as well as their literal composition and related multiple meanings. The title of the volume from which the story is taken is one such example: *Überseezungen*, a play on the German word *Übersetzung*, "translation," which sounds almost identical, albeit with a stressed third syllable, to "overseas tongues." The vivid, evocative compound noun *Mundhöhle*, captures an entirely different image, different connotations and interrelations than the English "mouth." Tawada's curiosity about words and her acuity in perceiving their hidden or inconspicuous meanings or underlying dimensions, which native speakers often fail to notice, constitute a central aspect in her writing. In an unedited online interview with Stanford professor Amir Eshel in 2009, Tawada pointed out that

> One reason why I write in German is it can be abstract, but even in the abstract word there is something very concrete [. . .] words like doubt, *Zweifel*, it's just one sound, you can't analyse it, the sound itself does not say what it is, but the German word *Zweifel*, it has in the sound what it means and also [. . .] it has the power how one word become two words or how we can cut one word in two parts [. . .] *Zwei—fel*, it's just one example how you can see in the abstract word some movement and materials . . .

To erase or level this intricate aspect of her writing is a questionable undertaking. According to Berman's analytic, the tendency of quantitative impoverishment refers to lexical loss—in the case of *Mundhöhle*, the loss of abundance of a text's unfixed signifiers. As he points out, "this loss perfectly coexists with an increase of the gross quantity or mass of the text with expansion" (292), another tendency conspicuously present in Bernofsky's rendition. Expansion, as a result of the translator's ambition to clarify (e.g., adverb, possessive pronoun) and rationalise (e.g., sentence structure) is, according to Berman, empty, as it only enlarges "the gross mass of text, without augmenting its way of speaking or signifying" (290). He adds that "addition is no more than babble designed to muffle the work's own voice [. . .] causing it to change from a shapeless plenitude to a shapeless void or hollow (290).

> When I wake up, my tongue is always somewhat swollen and much too large to move within the mouth's cavity.

The next sentence represents another example of explicative translation practice. Whereas the author senses an instance of pressure on her lungs (*ich spüre einen Druck auf die Lungen*), in Bernofsky's version pressure is building up: Tawada's *Atemweg*, "airway," becomes, in Bernofsky's translation, a "windpipe." The third sentence begins with a verbless, inserted question, which leads Bernofsky to add a verb, to render a grammatically incomplete, inconclusive statement complete and conclusive, or, in other words, a non-fluent sentence fluid, even though, evidently, Tawada has deliberately chosen to write a non-fluent, inconclusive sentence fragment. Furthermore, it seems questionable why Bernofsky has used the Greek word "esophagus" for gullet, or throat, when the original German text markedly abstains from scientific termini and instead uses colloquial German compounds: *Mundhöhle, Atemweg, Speiseröhre* (food tube). The paragraph ends with another expansion: *dabei nimmt sie meinen ganzen Kopf mit* in Bernofsky's version reads "dragging the rest of my head behind it." An alternative rendering of the remaining passage could read as follows:

> It obstructs my airways, I feel pressure on my lungs. How much longer, this suffocation? I ask myself, and at once it shrinks. My tongue reminds me of a used-up sponge, stiff and dry, it slowly retreats into my throat, while taking my whole head along with it.

III.ii.

Michael Hofmann's translation
of Herta Müller's *Herztier*

The opening chapter of *Herztier* (or *The Land of Green Plums*, its English title) consists of several short, sentence-length paragraphs. Herta Müller begins the novel with the programmatic sentence:

> Wenn wir schweigen, werden wir unangenehm, sagte Edgar, wenn wir reden, werden wir lächerlich.

Hofmann translates this sentence as follows:

> When we don't speak, said Edgar, we become unbearable, and when we do, we make fools of ourselves.

The translation reads coherently and seamlessly; the opening statement appears to be a simple, straightforward assertion. Yet a closer look at the mechanics, the texture of this sentence, reveals that the translator has in fact dissolved the underlying network of signification and instead created a seamless and polished, readable misrepresentation of the original.

The German *schweigen* is an active verb with no direct correspondent in English; it can mean to be, keep, or remain silent, quiet. Hofmann translates this verb in the form of a negative, "don't speak," which would be more consonant with the German phrase *nicht sprechen*. *Schweigen* and *nicht sprechen*, however, reflect and evoke two different states of mind. *Schweigen* "*ist keine Pause beim Reden, sondern eine Sache für sich*" (is not a pause in speaking, but a thing of its own) (**Müller,** *König* 74), particularly in Müller's word-scape, where the everpervasive, looming presence of silence reverberates consistently. In her omnipresent concern with the formation of her language and its origins in the life of the Banat village in which she grew up, *schweigen* is not simply pausing or not speaking or the absence of it, but rather a frame of mind, to remain silent and in one's own world, a stable, closed condition: "*Je mehr jemand zu schweigen imstande war, um so* *stärker war seine Präsenz"* (**Müller, König** 74) (the more someone was able to be silent, the stronger was his presence).

The next verb, *reden*, to "talk," in the follow-up conditional phrase *"wenn wir reden,"* forms an opposite pair, standing in opposition to the first verb *schweigen-reden*. Hofmann has, by translating it as "don't speak," deprived the text of this dualism, this dichotomy, its relational dimension, and instead employed a substitute, "do," as in "when we do." Inconsistently, in line seven, the translator employs the verbal phrase "to be silent" for the very verb *schweigen*, as in "Edgar was silent," *"Edgar schwieg."*

The German adjective *unangenehm*, Hofmann renders as "unbearable" in the English translation. *Unangenehm*, on the one hand, carries none of the vehemence or vigour expressed in the English word "unbearable"—the German word in back-translation would be closer to *unerträglich*. "Unpleasant," in contrast, has a more subtle and less obvious, a more artful and underhanded nuance. Edgar's statement has to be understood in the context of Müller's reception in West Germany after her emigration to West Berlin in 1987, in reference to her accounts of the regime's terror, of Ceausescu's atrocities. *"Das glaubt euch keiner, damit macht man sich nur lächerlich"* (No one will believe you, you're just going to make yourself look ridiculous), a friend advised her (**Müller, König** 103). Ideological alliances with revanchist quarters in the right-wing spectrum of politics were considered as unpresentable and uncouth, politically unsophisticated, her "truths" unpleasant, laughable, among the cosmopolitan, cultural elite in the West.

The translator concludes the paragraph with a figure of speech: "we make fools of ourselves." In Müller's text, by contrast, the last phrase, *werden wir lächerlich* (we become laughable), corresponds structurally and grammatically with the phrase *werden wir unangenehm: werden wir lächerlich* (we become laughable). The sentence structure has an almost mechanical, formulaic quality that is erased in Hofmann's translation—he provides an apt example of what Nabokov has flamboyantly called the substitution of "easy platitudes for the breathtaking intricacies of the text" (71). An alternative translation, following the original's articulation more sensitively, might read:

When we are silent, we become unpleasant, said Edgar, and when we talk, we become laughable.

According to Berman's analytical framework, Hofmann's translation exemplifies features of textual disfigurement for the sake of fluency. Firstly, he rearranges the sentence structure by moving forward the reported speech tag "said Edgar" with the aim, it must be assumed, to create a more fluid, perhaps even more rhythmical sentence, to "enhance the meaning" (Berman 291) in a stylistic exercise Berman describes as "ennoblement." The translator's attempts to rationalize the original sentence interfere with an inherent propensity in prose toward concreteness (289); his translation manoeuvres Müller's opening sentence into a contextual void. Secondly, as in Bernofsky's translation of Yoko Tawada, Hofmann demonstrates a tendency to reduce the abundance, the "proliferation of signifiers," in the original and obstructs the underlying networks of signification, for example, the textual correspondences. With the use of a more general vocabulary, a semantic levelling takes hold in that strongly marked or iconic words like *schweigen* are omitted or passed over, ignored.

The following paragraph builds on the imagery of the first:

> Mit den Wörtern im Mund zertreten wir so viel wie mit den Füßen im Gras. Aber auch mit dem Schweigen. (*Herztier* 7)

> The words in our mouths do as much damage as our feet on the grass. But so do our silences. (*Land* 1)

The verb Müller has chosen to describe the grim action in this image is *zertreten* "trample," a wilful, deliberate act, which again sharply contrasts with the flattened general register of Hofmann's version: "to do damage." According to Müller, the relevance of this "trampling" is not to be understood as an act of vandalism or "damage," but as the inability to communicate one's experiences (*König* 104). It appears to be a strategic approach of the translator to level distinctive idiosyncratic expressions and collocations by interpreting their possible meaning, thus blunting their metaphoric poignancy.

In her reflections on *Herztier* during a *Poetikdozentur*, a lecture series at the University of Tübingen in 2001, Müller elaborated the context of the previously discussed word "laughable" (*König* 102): being unable to relate the horrors of seeing a drowned body, bound with wire, covered in mud on a pauper's field because she was warned that it would be received as a confabulation. The grasses in the cemetery develop an uncanny metonymic relationship with the murders, the drowned, bound bodies she links with the regime, with the unbelievable, incommunicable:

> With the words in our mouth we trample as much as with our feet on the grass.

The last paragraph of this introductory chapter rounds up this imagery and brings it to a preliminary denouement:

> Das Gras steht im Kopf. Wenn wir reden, wird es gemäht. Aber auch, wenn wir schweigen. Und das zweite, dritte Gras wächst nach, wie es will. Und dennoch haben wir Glück. (*Herztier* 8)

> The grass stands tall inside our heads. When we speak it gets mowed. Even when we don't. And then the second, and the third growth springs up at will. And still: We are the lucky ones. (*Land* 2)

It is impossible, "laughable," to put into words the experience of terror; it is as inarticulate as silence. The verb "stand" doesn't refer to maturity or a growing process but to being present, motionless. The grass stands inside the head. The atrocities, the system, the dictatorship, in Müller's frame of mind, continue, unchecked, unstoppable, and glad are those who survive.

> The grass stands inside the head. When we talk it gets mowed. But also, when we are silent. And the second, third grass grows back, all at will. And yet we are lucky.

In her writing, objects are kept at a distance, they can't form relationships, the "grass in the head" or the "words in the mouth" being fitting examples. She does not refer to her head as a head of a shared
commonality; objects are multifarious entities: "*Daselbe Taschentuch
ist nie das gleiche. Wie viele nicht gesagte Möglichkeiten gibt es in dem
so einfach klingenden Satz: Die Frau steckt ihr Taschentuch ein*" (The
handkerchief is never the same. How many unuttered possibilities lie
in the simple-sounding sentence: The woman puts her handkerchief
into her pocket) (*König* 89).

In the last translated excerpt Hofmann again seems to magnify or
reinforce—to touch up—Müller's sparse, terse prose. The first short
sentence in Hofmann's paragraph has the grass stand "tall inside our
heads." Formally speaking, Müller's sentence is unadorned and gruff,
stylistically plain, somewhat naïve, *Das Gras steht im Kopf* (the grass
stands in the head). In his objective to render the original fluent, Hofmann's poetic urges or ambitions impose themselves on Müller's text,
deforming the laconic, stilted texture by building a syntactic coherence on the surface structure that the original decidedly eschews.

It would be a pedantic exercise to emphasize and criticize in minutia
instances of potential mistranslations when analysing and evaluating
translations or, similarly, to demand a translator be knowledgeable
about every nuance, the complete background of the text or the writer's palette—losses and misses are an inevitable presence in writing as
in translating. The aim here, rather, is to take a closer look at the working patterns of accomplished, published translators and to scrutinize
the underlying rationale of naturalizing, indeed neutralizing an original text in translation, thus interfering adversely with the original's
composition, its complexity, its aesthetic raison d'être.

The difficulties of following and articulating the intricacies of a
source text and its references are confounded by language norms, conventions, and etiquettes that "native" translators seemed to be explic-
itly bound up in, an interpretive act entirely anchored in and directed
at the receiving culture. In a recent interview in the translation journal
Two Lines, Bernofsky elaborated that "as a writer and translator I've
learned to write English as fluidly as possible—after all, that's what

good style is all about—but too much fluidity kills these [Tawada's] texts. Of course, if they come out sounding awkward and wooden, that would also be deadly!" Her allusions concerning the death of a text in translation do not refer to the erasure of the original's texture but are oriented toward the translation's readability, that is, a smooth, digestible American English version of a text deprived of its linguistic centre. The somewhat simplistic positioning of her working objective as a middle-of-the-road approach is certainly not confirmed by her translation of Yoko Tawada's "*Zungentanz.*" Quite on the contrary, the underlying rationale in her translation, as that of Hofmann's efforts, is her proclaimed "good style," revealing a consistent, systematic pattern that is uncannily reminiscent of Tytler's transfusion: the ease of original composition.

PUBLISHERS AT WORK

Publishing trends and perspectives on translations are not principally based on aesthetic considerations or values but closely bound to economic and political realities and constraints, in particular to the impact that given cultures and languages exert on others. In the case of the ascendancy of English (or Englishes, in view of the multitude of English variants across the globe) as a global language, it has propelled Anglophone publishing into a position of power and supremacy. Responding to this ominous trend, Phillipson, an outspoken critic of the impact of global English on "minor" languages, formulated the term linguistic imperialism (Phillipson, 1992). Other translation theorists such as Venuti or Campbell have discussed translating into English in the context of linguistic or cultural hegemony. In his history of translation, for example, Lawrence Venuti observed that Anglo-American publishers have produced a reading culture that is "aggressively monolingual, unreceptive to foreign literature, accustomed to fluent translations that invisibly inscribe foreign texts with British and American values and provide readers with the narcissistic experience of recognizing their own culture in a cultural other" (12). The dominance of English on a global scale appears to have promoted the advance of a literary monoculture in the United States and United Kingdom, embedding a self-sufficient intellectual parochialism that is glaringly reflected in the output of the British and American publishing industries.

Three Percent, a resource for international literature at the University of Rochester "was named after the oft-cited statistic that only 3% of books published in the U.S. are translations" (*Three Percent*). This figure is widely confirmed and reiterated in recent publications on translations. In her short book *Why Translation Matters* (2010), the acclaimed translator Edith Grossmann complains that "in English-speaking nations, major commercial publishers are strangely resistant to publishing literary translations" and "statistics indicate that in the US and the UK, for example, only two to three percent of books published each year are literary translations" (28).

According to the University of Rochester's painstakingly collected data concerning new book releases, about 0.7% of all books published in 2009 in the United States, 358 books in total were prose or poetry titles in translation. To put this figure in perspective, the Frankfurt Book Fair's journal *Ueber:blick* reported that in 2009, 2,851 books of fiction in translation were published in the German book market (Wischenbart 21), the number referring exclusively to translations from English, whereas the US figure above refers to all languages translated into English. This staggering misbalance is by no means atypical, (in fact, German, after French, is the second-most translated source language) but represents the state of Anglo-American publishing on a global scale.

The reluctance to translate and publish foreign literatures has produced a dissociated literary landscape in the so-called inner circle Anglophone cultures, in the United States, United Kingdom, Australia or New Zealand. This impasse potentially divorces the English readership from non-English philosophical, literary and cultural dispositions and developments, depriving the reading public of a sophisticated perspective of a world they are, after all, a part of: "The American reader seems to be largely disengaged from literatures in other languages, which many see as yet another symptom of culturally catastrophic American isolationism," Aleksandar Hemon wrote in his introduction to *Best European Fiction 2010* (15). This institutionalised indifference vis-à-vis foreign literatures and cultures in turn generates and fosters translational and editorial objectives and practice that are astonishingly uninformed and ignorant and tends to subordinate foreign literatures to suit domestic literary standards, the perceived "taste" of the public.

Of the rare accounts available on editing procedures from the coalface of the publishing industry, the following comments reveal the prevailing modus operandi. Reflecting on his experience editing Giovanni Pontiero's acclaimed translation of José Saramago's *History of the Siege of Lisbon*, Guido Waldmann of Harvill Press illustrated the rationale surrounding editorial interference. The overall problem, he noted, "lies less with the rendering into English than with the source text itself . . . a foreign author's inadequacies" (Waldmann 95). Paradoxically, the editor revealed that "having myself no grasp of the source language, I had to concern myself principally with how the text read in English" (Waldmann 95). In this monolingual universe, the focus of the editorial work is reduced to an absurd, Kafkaesque assessment of the English "original," with a problematic foreign language version somewhere in the background, invisible, irrelevant, and at best a nuisance to the editor. Following the tenor of Tytler's translation maxims, Waldmann (95) continued that "I would look for an inner coherence and so long as this appeared to me seamless, I would assume that the translation was faithful." It is obvious that this preposterous view of translation, an evaluation of the merits of a translated text based entirely on the translating language, is, especially from a publishing point of view, utterly unacceptable—it deprives the translation of its essential quality: the mediation, the retrieval of the foreign.

Robyn Marsack, a distinguished editor with Carcanet Press who worked on the translation into English of Clarice Lispector, expressed a similarly embarrassing attitude about the original author ("sheer disbelief that writers can get away with the things they seem to in their native language"; 99) and the same incompetence in evaluating the source language ("I write from the perspective of an editor without Portuguese who was concerned to make the books readable in English"). Marsack elaborated further:

> I defended my inclination to make one sentence out of two where the second began with a participle; otherwise it seemed so ungrammatical in English. While I realized that this and other alterations to punctuation had the effect of making the structure more conventional, the book seemed so strange that removing a few obstacles did not constitute a great betrayal.
>
> (103)

The author, unless she is able to assess the translating language vis-à-vis the source, has no voice in this process. Marsack's working ethics are reminiscent of Tytler's "good taste" when he praised Pope's translation of Homer for having concealed or covered up the Greek's tendencies "to offend, by introducing low images and puerile allusions. Yet

how admirably is this defect veiled over, or altogether removed ... "
(Tytler 82).

The principal tenet of publishing practices, especially in the Anglophone world, is to ensure that a translation reads naturally, fluently, seamlessly; the objective is to sanitize and absorb it according to vague, static notions of readability, to enforce the absence of any nonstandard stylistic traits. It is an approach in perfect congruity with the much lauded "cultural turn" of translation studies in the 1980s, hailed as a change of paradigm, "ground breaking contributions," according to Snell-Hornby (Turns 47), which focused on the function of the translation in the target culture: "descriptive, target-oriented, functional and systemic" (49). The new orientation in translation studies was, however, obviously a mere rehash of the fluidity continuum that has dominated the praxis of literary translations from Cicero to the present.

"It would certainly make me laugh," Milan Kundera (319) conceded in the afterword to the fifth edition in 1992 of his first novel *The Joke* in English translation, "if it didn't concern me." Competent to read and evaluate the translation vis-à-vis the Czech original—in sharp contrast to most Anglophone editors—Kundera didn't recognise his novel at all when he received the first 1969 English version by David Hamblyn and Oliver Stalybrass: "the novel was entirely reconstructed; divided into a different number of parts, with chapters shortened or simply omitted" (319). A protest letter he published in the *Times Literary Supplement* achieved a revised, "complete" translation by Penguin in 1970, which, nonetheless, also showed strong interferences on closer inspection: "Helena's monologue ... in which each paragraph is one long 'infinite' [sic] sentence in my original, had been broken up into many short sentences. I decided to close the book and know no more of it" (320). In the third edition, the American counterpart published at about the same time by Coward-McCann in New York, the text was "systematically curtailed." The first two paragraphs, for instance, consisted of seventy-two lines in the "complete" Penguin version, but in the American print, only fifteen had survived the editorial censorship (Kundera 320). Several years later Kundera's new editor at Harper & Row proposed to publish *The Joke* at last in a faithful, unabridged version, and so the fourth English translation was commissioned. The translator Michael Henry Heim, in a show of ambitious support for Kundera's oeuvre, had translated and published, in a literary journal, the omitted parts from the first edition and thereby won Kundera's trust. The fourth version of *The Joke* was published in 1982, and Kundera, without having properly examined the text, introduced it in his preface: "now the same professor of literature who ten years ago published the material omitted from the English edition has done the first valid and authentic version of a book that tells of rape and has itself so often been violated." And so finally, or so it seemed, the ultimate, approved text appeared in the Harper & Row rendition. When Kundera was approached by the same publisher about a republication in 1990 he decided to review the Heim translation this time around:

> In the beginning there was nothing seriously wrong, and Part Two, "Helena," was quite good, but from the start of Part Three, I had the increasingly strong impression that what I read was not my text: often the words were remote from what I had written; the syntax differed too; there was inaccuracy of all the reflective passages; irony had been transformed into satire; unusual turns of phrase had been obliterated; the distinctive voices of the character-narrators had been altered to the extent of altering their personalities (thus Ludvik, that thoughtful, melancholy intellectual, became vulgar and cynical). I was all the more unhappy because I did not believe that it was a matter of incompetence on the translator's part, or of carelessness or ill will: no; in good conscience he had produced the kind of translation that one might call translation-adaptation (adaptation to the taste of the time and of the country for which it was intended, to the taste, in the final analysis, of the translator). Is this the current normal practice? It's possible. But unacceptable. Unacceptable to me. (322)

In the end, Kundera meticulously reworked the English text in word-for-word translations of the original when it was necessary, in English or French, retaining acceptable renderings and phrases from the previous work by Heim and Hamblyn and Stallybrass. He sent his corrections to his editor who created from them an English-language version that he sent back to Kundera for final approval. The fifth and ultimate version was published in 1992 with the solemn promise by the author that there would not be a sixth.

The aesthetic values of a dominant culture can be so controlling and pervasive, as another notorious example demonstrates, that the writer consciously or subconsciously submits to its dictates, an act of self-denial inspired, in this case, by the cultural legacy of British colonialism. Mehasweta Sengupta examined the self-translations by Rabindranath Tagore from Bengali into English of his collection *Gitanjali*, for which he won the Nobel Prize for Literature in 1913. In comparing one of Tagore's poems originally written in Bengali with the same poem in his English translation, she noticed that "Tagore changes not only the style of the original but also the imagery and tone of the lyric, not to mention the register of language which is made to match the target-language poetics of Edwardian English" (57). While Tagore's writing in Bengali was stimulated by the spoken word, by oral narrative traditions, in translation the British subject emulated his colonial master. Even the selection of poems for the translated anthology furthered Tagore's acculturation with themes of an apparently mystical, spiritual nature, thereby accommodating perceived expectations and tastes of the English-speaking target audience: "the only way in which the coloniser was prepared to deal with the colonised, the only possible ground for admitting one from the subject race, who is accepted because he represents the wisdom and exoticism of the 'other' world" (Sengupta 61).

These incidents of editorial rationale correspond with the larger picture pervading Anglophone translational praxis. It is critical to reconsider the ingrained tendencies and traditions that are determining the face and objectives of literary translations in English. An acute, profound understanding of translating and translated languages and culture is an imperative prerequisite to identify and retrieve the stylistic features that constitute the aesthetic and cultural framework of the original. A creative sensibility toward an appreciation of the original's imprint on the translating language is indispensible for translator and editor alike, in order that they refrain from unreflecting, trivial attitudes and approaches that diminish or obscure the original. The endemic monolingualism in American or British cultural institutions calls for a challenge, a sea change for new, different directions in literary translations to emerge. It is with considerable authority that Gayatri Chakravorty Spivak stipulated: "You cannot translate from a position of monolinguist superiority" (410).

New Directions

> Ich ekelte mich oft vor Menschen, die fließend ihre Mutter-
> sprache sprachen. Sie machten den Eindruck, dass sie nichts
> anderes denken und spüren konnten als das, was ihre Sprache
> ihnen so schnell und bereitwillig anbietet.
>   —Yoko Tawada, (*Talisman* 42)

I was disgusted by people who spoke their mother tongue fluently. They gave the impression that they were incapable of
thinking and feeling anything else than what their language so
instantly and willingly provides.

In tandem with the staunchly engraved fluency rule, there seems to
be a tacit, unanimous understanding among English translation pro-
fessionals that literature translated into a second or non-native language is a fraught, unacceptable proposition. Meta Grosman, co-edi-
tor of *Translation into Non-Mother Tongues*, warned that where literary
translation is concerned "the demand for quality and/or successful
functioning permits no consideration of non-native speakers when
the translation is to be published for target readers, or rather, in the
target culture" (25). The fraternity holds that translations into a second language inevitably read unnaturally and awkwardly, are hounded by ungrammatical and un-colloquial interferences from the mother tongue. Beverly Adabs, in phrasing the question at hand in the
more conciliatory tone of the sociolinguist, wonders

> whether the translator as a member of the source language
> community, is able, when mapping source language concepts
> into target language frames, to adopt the target language per-
> spectives or whether there is still some degree of interference
> from his/her own mother tongue and source culture which
> will impede successful completion of the cognitive aspects of
> the process. (230)

Notwithstanding the universal consensus on the concepts of the mother tongue or first language, the immediate relevance of this label has become difficult to ascertain. Considering that large parts of the world outside the Anglophone sphere are in fact bi- or multilingual and that an ever-increasing global mobility drastically impacts on both foreign and domestic language(s), a preliminary definition can at best establish that a first language or languages is/are acquired from birth and that second languages are consciously learned at a later stage in life—the mother tongue does not automatically denote primacy over second or third languages. In fact, the notion of mother tongue as a static, stagnant value is inadequate in determining proficiency or originality in a given language. Global migrations that have led to postcolonial and cross-cultural encounters and interactions have produced comprehensive shifts in language usage: The replacement of the mother tongue by the second languages, its modification, regression or decline have led to hybrid languages or nonstandard forms. And "even when one has only a single mother tongue," Jacques Derrida proposed in conversation with Évelynne Grossman, "when one is rooted in the place of one's birth and in one's language, even then language is not owned . . . Language is precisely what does not let itself be possessed but, for this very reason, provokes all kinds of movements of appropriation" (101). It appears that the concept of "mother tongue" is first and foremost an ideological construct and far less instrumental with regard to language sensibility and creativity in a second language. It is persuasive, however, in its extra-linguistic applications: as an ethnocentric instrument of control, dominance and discrimination in colonial and post-colonial contexts, in dissociating foreign languages and cultures, as a guarantor for language competence in the demarcation of exclusive belonging and ownership; and as a lever excluding language varieties considered substandard.

The designation native speaker is equally simplistic, defined as a fixed, stable entity, an innate, authoritative competence—being a native speaker, as its benchmark usage in linguistics and translation studies implies, represents the highest level of linguistic proficiency and in-depth cultural knowledge, as if language was uniform and linguistic fragmentation, disruption and deficiencies were not frequent, inherent facets of language. If class and ethnicity within a given language community—if socio-cultural, psychological and educational determiners and backgrounds are taken into account—the native speaker dictum becomes evidently flawed and ineffective, its guarantee of a preeminent language standard untenable. According to current definitions, Józef T. K. Korzeniowski, or Joseph Conrad, never came even close to native speaker status—Ford Madox Ford felt he "had so strong a French (sic!) accent that few who did not know him well could understand him at first" (Pokorn 8)—and yet, the apparently inarticulate Pole with the heavy accent wrote himself into the pantheon of English literature in, it has to be pointed out, his fourth language. As far as accomplishment and aptitude of non-native speakers are concerned, the authors in this anthology are conclusive proof that creativity, depth and expertise in writing are not confined to the domain of the native writer or mother tongue speaker.

Still, the tentative, emerging discourse of language direction in literary translation is hampered and frustrated by the ubiquitous doctrine of mother tongue supremacy, unequivocally assumed and rigorously enforced by the profession. As Beeby Lonsdale (64) observed: "direct translation as the only viable professional option is particularly dominant in English-speaking countries." Research-based evidence on the subject of directionality is, however, scarce and the few publications available are mainly concerned with methodological considerations in the context of translator training (see Grosman, Kadric, Kovačič, Snell-Hornby 2000). Stuart Campbell's substantial contribution in the field of inverse translation, for instance, is limited to developing and promoting a teaching framework for the translation of non-literary texts into a second language, the reason being pragmatic: the increased economic demand in areas of high migrant populations (Campbell 1998).

The first comprehensive study to look specifically at the reception of native and non-native literary translations among an Anglophone readership was published by Nike K. Pokorn in 2005. In her study, the author sampled American and Canadian English native speakers with academic backgrounds in the humanities to evaluate English translations of the Slovenian writer Ivan Cankar by native, non-native, or

pair translators. The study produced a number of discerning and challenging results; one of the main findings contradicts the conventional
belief in the inferiority of inverse translation: Only about 60% of the
mother tongue respondents identified correctly whether a given translation passage was written by a native or a non-native translator (Pokorn
112). The result cast doubt on the obstinate and all-pervasive premise
that translations written by non-native speakers of a given language
are by necessity flawed, substandard and patently transparent to the
native reader and disputes

> the concept of an ideal native speaker as an arbiter and model
> of grammaticality, who masters his/her mother tongue com-
> pletely and in all its detail, who has access to all the hidden
> channels of unutterable associative connectedness between
> words and concepts, and can therefore also create linguistical-
> ly and culturally impeccable translations. (Pokorn 27)

This particular outcome is even more striking if the recognition mark-
ers for the translations are considered. The evaluation criteria of the
respondents—without, it has to be assumed, knowledge of the source
language or recourse to a critical theoretical framework—centred entirely on impressions of fluency and colloquial or idiomatic standards
in the target language. The findings suggest that, even judged by the
conservative standards of a monolingual readership attuned to normative language conventions, non-native translators are capable of pro-
ducing translations to the same degree of acceptability with which native speakers are, by and large, regarded. Not surprisingly, there was
almost unanimity concerning the ideal translation strategy, with 86%
of the interviewees opting for a target audience-oriented or fluency
approach (116).

Another finding revealed that almost 20% of the respondents considered the only native English translator in the sample, Henry Leeming (a teacher at the Slavonic department of London University), who
has no Slovene cultural background or affiliations, to be, intriguingly,
a non-native English speaker (110). This result is of course, remarkable,
particularly as Leeming's overall approach to the text is, as Pokorn (66)

attests, characterized by fluency strategies, "from changes of punctuation and paragraphs, omissions and changes to meaning. For example, Leeming consistently shortens Cankar's paragraphs and sentences and thus also changes the author's characteristic style." The reasoning behind the respondents' evaluation of Leeming is stereotypical:

- "Reads like a translation. Typical of a romantic novel."
- "The expressions are odd: 'that face', 'she never'. Note the errors: 'as if she was' (it should be 'were'), the wrong use of punctuation."
- "Perhaps it is simply awkward. The word 'to smart' is very dictionary."
- "The word 'to smart' is too bookish."
- "The translator was influenced by Hemingway. American influence."
- "Idioms are all correct. The use of 'sister' at that point seems to me very un-English."
- "Instinct rather than rational thought."
- "'Furrowed with tears' is not American English; 'the eyes' is not expected, it should be 'her eyes'; 'come away' should be 'leave.'"
- "The expression 'Is she never going to come away from here again?' did not sound like it was written by a native English speaker." (Pokorn 142)

The respondents' comments reveal a prescriptive appraisal of the translations, detecting and rejecting features that appear unusual, nonstandard or are considered audaciously foreign and deviant. It almost appears as if not the original text but the English language, its "original cultural identity" (Snell Hornby, *McLanguage* 36), is at stake and has to be rescued and cleansed from the contaminations of a perverted hybrid language. On another plane the responses demonstrate a fundamental flaw in Pokorn's otherwise laudable study: despite the critique of the notions of mother tongue and native speaker she applies and unintentionally perpetuates the misconception that monolingual readers with academic credentials (13 BAs, 15 MAs, 18 PhDs) are unequivocally qualified to evaluate the merits or shortcomings of translated literature. The assessment is based on the (monolingual) understanding that a translation has to be readable and fluid and that it has to remain unaffected by its source text, a premise as meaningless and irrelevant as it is ideological and dogmatic.

Leeming's "jarring lines," despite employing predictable native speaker strategies overall (Pokorn 100), are evocative. There is an aspect of the inherent motion of translation broached here, irrespective of Leeming's actual intentions or aptitude: At the interface, the exchange between two languages, the bilingual translator is in a position to inhabit an external perspective on both languages, to be responsive and sensitised to the translating and the translated language in almost equal measure. At the stage of its articulation into another, the source language potentially asserts itself and imprints on the translating language, a motion that is far more incisive for the non-native translator—it resembles a crucial facet of writing in a foreign language as, for instance, the incongruities encountered by Yoko Tawada have indicated. Both the first and the second language appear estranged and unwieldy—effortless, automatic lapses into prefabricated language structures are obstructed, standard phrasing and patterning latently undermined. At the interstice of languages, interruptions occur, fixtures become porous, polarities appear less secure and the translator retrieves features of the original, strange or jarring once the "interim" encounter is cancelled.

In this light, Prunč (9) mediated a more plausible understanding of the mother tongue/native speaker nexus, suggesting that language competence and creative potential in a multilingual speaker can be apportioned or divided between different languages. He contends that bilingualism and biculturalism are subject to permanent fluctuations dependent upon contact with the culture concerned, and, most importantly, he asserts that language competence of bilingual speakers or writers, regardless of a primary- or secondary-language acquisition process, has to be understood as a temporally variable continuum in which either language can occupy a dominant position (10).

The interchangeability, the temporal shifts in prominence of first or second languages, does not negate their different status and the subjective significance they embody for the writer or the translator.

The distinctions or peculiarities of first or second languages depend on the translator's approach to writing, her/his affiliations and literary sensibilities, her/his sense of acculturation. The "foreign" translator working into her/his second language is tempted to approach the first language as a source, an archive, a repository that is sedentary, settled, while the second language is in flux, plastic, less encumbered or conditioned by assignations and purposes. Working into the second as the translating language facilitates a reading that is not primarily fixed on the surface content of a text and its reception but follows the underlying mapping and aesthetic design of the original work in the way it frames writing and traces its inquiries. This is the working proposition, the role the Spanish philosopher Ortega y Gasset had assigned for literary translation when he claimed that "the translation is not the work, but the path toward the work" (61) — the translation depends on and presupposes the original to remain foreign: We need the original texts, as he further elaborates, "precisely to the degree they are dissimilar to us." (62)

In a similar vein, Antoine Berman claimed that "translation is a trial of the foreign . . . by aiming to open up the foreign work to us in its utter foreignness," and that "translation is a trial for the foreign as well, since the foreign work is uprooted from its own *language-ground*" (284). This uprootedness manifests itself most distinctly, transparently, in translating from the first language, a mode of translating with its own propositions, with its own tendencies. The "foreign" translator is by necessity closer to, inherently invested in the original, less inclined or adept to employ normalizing strategies, less tempted to clarify, and instead drawn to articulate the inconclusiveness, the arbitrariness of the original, to trace and extend its motion of *Sprachfindung*, its search for language in the translating language. The metaphor of *übersetzen*, *übertragen*, "to carry over, across," reveals this integral movement, illustrates the distinction between the foreign and the native approach: In the latter, the translator pulls the language over to her/his native language; the foreign translator, however, moves with the original, is carried across with it to new language grounds. The ubiquitous notion of "good style" and "fluidity" so prevalent in contemporary translation practice coincides with the directionality maxim that translators are to work into their first language—its ambition to dress up or re-dress the original text, an overwriting that represents itself as the "original." The foreign translator, in contrast, is not as constricted or bound by the scaffolds of language conventions that constitute readability or similar prescriptive aesthetic principles. Working from the first language seems to facilitate a hesitation in the space of insignificance, an awareness of the text's instability and potential. In the interstice of languages, the foreign translator tends to lean, to drift back toward, and to be guided by the original; the translating language does not as easily develop its own momentum, that is, its own banalities for the sake of readability.

Writing as distinctly accentuated and articulated, as in the prose texts assembled for the present anthology, requires minimal imprints and impositions on the part of the translator. It is essential to settle into the text's rhythms and tempos, its narrative threading, its tonality, to follow and to make comprehensible, if only fragmentarily and provisionally, the original's representation, its undertone, its force and effect. There is an interstice between languages, where translation pauses, where elusiveness and incompatibility, a momentary volatility of imagery and texture, lie bare; it is an instant of "insignificance," of indecision, a fixture not quite released and not yet reassembled, an uncertainty. This is the place where the text is set, the original constituted as an original, created vis-à-vis the translation. Translation is about this place; it is the text and also the manifestation of the text, its retrieval and its documentation.

Works Cited

PRIMARY SOURCES

Benjamin, Walter. *Gesammelte Schriften IV.I.* Frankfurt: Suhrkamp Verlag, 1972. Print.

Bodrožić, Marica. *Sterne erben, Sterne färben. Meine Ankunft in Wörtern.* Frankurt am Main: Suhrkamp Verlag, 2007. Print.

Celan, Paul. *Gesammelte Werke 3. Band.* Frankfurt am Main: Suhrkamp Verlag, 1983. Print.

Frisch, Max. *Gesammelte Werke, Tagebuch 1966-1971, Band VI.* Frankfurt am Main: Suhrkamp, 1976. Print.

Kundera, Milan. *The Joke.* London: Faber and Faber, 1992. Print.

Müller, Herta. *Der König verneigt sich und tötet.* München: Carl Hanser Verlag, 2003. Print.

—. *Herztier.* 5th ed. Frankfurt am Main: Fischer Verlag 2009. Print.

Tawada, Yoko. *Talisman.* Tübingen: Konkursbuchverlag, 1996. Print.

—. *Überseezungen.* Tübingen: Konkursbuchverlag, 2003. Print.

Zaimoglu, Feridun. *Kanak Sprak.* Hamburg: Rotbuch Verlag, 1995. Print.

SECONDARY SOURCES

Aciman, Andre. *Letters of Transit: Reflections of Exile and Memory.* New York: The New Press, 2000. Print.

Adabs, Beverly. "Translating into a Second Language: Can We, Should We?" *In and out of English: For Better or For Worse?* Eds. Gunilla Anderman and Margaret Rogers. Clevedon: Multilingual Matter, 2005. 227–241. Print.

Alms, Barbara. "Fremdheit als ästhetisches Prinzip. Zu den deutschsprachigen Romanen der Tschechin Libuše Moníková." *Stint* 6 (1989): 138–151. Print.

Bassnett-McGuire, Susan. *Translation Studies.* London: Methuen, 1980. Print.
Beeby Lonsdale, Allison. "Directionality." *Encyclopedia of Translation Studies.* Ed. Mona Baker. London: Routledge, 1998. 84–88. Print.

Benjamin, Walter. *Illuminations.* Trans. Harry Zohn. London: Fontana Press, 1992. Print.

Berman, Antoine. "Translation and the Trials of the Foreign." *The Translation Studies Reader.* Ed. Lawrence Venuti. London: Routledge, 2000. 284–297. Print.

Bernofsky, Susan. "Susan Bernofsky on Yoko Tawada's *The Naked Eye.*" *Two Words: The Blog of the Center for the Art of Translation.* The Center for the Art of Translation, 30 July 2009. Web. 3 Mar. 2011.

Biondi, Franco. "Die Fremde wohnt in der Sprache." *Eine nicht nur deutsche Literatur.* Eds. Irmgard Ackermann and Harald Weinrich. München: Piper, 1986. 25–32. Print.

Biondi, Franco and Schami, Rafik. "Literatur der Betroffenheit." *Zu Hause in der Fremde*. Ed. Christian Schaffernicht. Fischerhude: Verlag Atelier im Bauernhaus, 1981. 124–135. Print.

Braunbeck, Helga, G. "Gespräche mit Libuse Monikova 1992–1997." *Monatshefte* 89.4 (1997): 452–467. Web. 13 Oct. 2010.

Campbell, Stuart. *Translation into the Second Language*. New York: Longman, 1998. Print.

Chiellino, Gino. "Die Fremde als Ort der Geschichte." *Eine nicht nur deutsche Literatur*. Eds. Irmgard Ackermann and Harald Weinrich. München: Piper, 1986. 13–16. Print.

—. *Literatur und Identität in der Fremde*. Kiel: Neuer Malik Verlag, 1989. Print.

Cicero, Tullius, Marcus. *De inventione: de optimo genere oratorum*. Trans. H. M. Hubell, London: Heinemann, 1968. Print.

Copeland, Rita. *Rhetoric, Hermeneutics, and Translation in the Middle Ages*. Cambridge: Cambridge University Press, 1991. Print.

—. "The Fortunes of 'non verbum pro verbo': or, Why Jerome is Not a Ciceronian." *The Medieval Translator*. Ed. Roger Ellis. Cambridge: D.S. Brewer, 1989. 15–35. Print.

Dal, Güney. "Chronik der Auswanderung." *Eine nicht nur deutsche Literatur*. Eds. Irmgard Ackermann, and Harald Weinrich. München: Piper, 1986. 16–17. Print.

Derrida, Jacques. "Language is Never Owned: An Interview." *Sovereignties in Question: The Poetics of Paul Celan*. Eds. Thomas Dutoit and Outi Pasanen. New York: Fordham University Press, 2005. 97–107. Print.

Filip, Ota. "Leseprobe." *Ota Filip*. *Adalbert-von-Chamisso-Preis 1986*. Robert Bosch Stiftung, n.d. Web. 14. Jan. 2010.

Frey, Hans-Jost. "Übersetzung als Metapher." *Vom Glück sich anzustecken. Möglichkeiten und Risiken im Übersetzungsprozess*. Ed. Martin A. Hainz. Wien: Braunmüller, 2005. 39–43. Print.

Geiser, Myriam. "'Der Konkurrenz eine Sprache voraus': Sprachmigration in der Gegenwartsliteratur mit einem vergleichenden Blick nach Frankreich." *In mehreren Sprachen leben. Literaturwissenschaftliche, sprachdidaktische und sprachwissenschaftliche Aspekte der Mehrsprachigkeit*. Eds. Daniel Grabis and Eva Kastenhuber. Trier: Universität Trier, 2006. 59–92. Print.

Grosman, Meta. "Non-Mother Tongue Translation: An Open Challenge." *Translation into Non-Mother Tongues*. Eds. Meta Grosman, Mira Kadric, Irena Kovačič and Mary Snell-Hornby. Tübingen: Stauffenburg Verlag, 2000. 21–33. Print.

Grossman, Edith. *Why Translation Matters*. New Haven: Yale University Press, 2010. Print.

Gutjahr, Jacqueline. "Einladung zum Spiel—den Texten von Yoko Tawada auf der Spur." *In mehreren Sprachen leben. Literaturwissenschaftliche, sprachdidaktische und sprachwissenschaftliche Aspekte der Mehrsprachigkeit.* Eds. Daniel Grabis and Eva Kastenhuber. Trier: Universität Trier, 2006. 21–42. Print.

Gwynn, Aubrey. *Roman Education from Cicero to Quintilian.* Oxford: Clarendon Press, 1926. Print.

Handke, Peter. "Eine herbstliche Reise zu Peter Handke nach Paris." *Die Zeit Online* 1 Dec. 2010, Literatur. Web. 10 Dec. 2010.

Hein-Khatib, Simone. *Sprachmigration und literarische Kreativität.* Frankfurt am Main: Peter Lang Europäischer Verlag der Wisenschaften, 1998. Print.

Hemon, Aleksandar, ed. *Best European Fiction 2010.* London: Dalkey Archive Press, 2010. Print.

Herbert, Ulrich. *Geschichte der Ausländerpolitik in Deutschland: Saison-arbeiter, Zwangsarbeiter, Gastarbeiter, Flüchtlinge.* München: Beck, 2001. Print.

Hermans, Theo. "The Task of the Translator in the European Renaissance." *Translating Literature.* Ed. Susan Bassnett. Cambridge: Brewer, 1997. 14–40. Print.

Hieronymi, D. "De optimo genere interpretandi." *Opera Omnes Quae Extant.* Basileae, 1536. Print.

Jacobs, Carol. *In the Language of Walter Benjamin.* Baltimore: John Hopkins University Press, 1999. Print.

Jerome. "Letter to Pammachius." Trans. Kathleen Davis, in *The Translation Studies Reader.* Ed. Lawrence Venuti. 2nd ed. London: Routledge, 2004. 21–31. Print.

Knowlson, James. *Damned to Fame: The Life of Samuel Beckett.* London: Bloomsbury, 1997. Print.

Lefevere, André. "Translation: its Genealogy in the West." *Translation, History and Culture.* Eds. Susan Bassnett and André Lefevere. London: Pinter, 1990. 14–29. Print.

Marrou, Henri Irénée. *The History of Education in Antiquity.* Trans. George Lamb. New York: New American Library, 1964. Print.

Marsack, Robyn. "Discovering the Word." *The Translator's Dialogue.* Eds. Pilar Orero and Juan C Sager. Amsterdam: John Benjamins, 1997. 99–106. Print.

Müller, Herta. *The Land of Green Plums.* Trans. Michael Hofmann. New York: Metropolitan Books, 1996. Print.

Nabokov, Vladimir. "Problems of Translation: 'Onegin' in English." *The Translation Studies Reader.* Ed. Lawrence Venuti. London: Routledge, 2000. 71–83. Print.

Naoum, Jusuf. "Aus dem Ghetto heraus." *Eine nicht nur deutsche Literatur.* Eds. Irmgard Ackermann and Harald Weinrich. München: Piper, 1986. 79–81. Print.

Ortega y Gasset, José. "The Misery and Splendor of Translation." Trans. Elizabeth Gamble Miller. *The Translation Studies Reader*. Ed. Lawrence Venuti. London: Routledge, 2000. 49–63. Print.

Osers, Ewald. "Translation Norms: Do They Really Exist?" *Translators' Strategies and Creativity*. Eds. Ann Beylard-Ozeroff, Jana Králová and Barbara Moser-Mercer. Amsterdam: John Benjamins, 1995. 53–62. Print.

Phillipson, Robert. *Linguistic Imperialism*. Oxford: Oxford University Press, 1992. Print.

Pokorn, Nike K. *Challenging the Traditional Axiom*. Amsterdam: John Benjamins Publishing, 2005. Print.

Pratt, Karen. "Medieval Attitudes to Translation and Adaptation: Rhetorical Theory and Poetic Practice." *The Medieval Translator II*. Ed. Roger Ellis. London: Centre for Medieval Studies, University of London, 1991. 1–27. Print.

Prunč, Erich. "Translation in die Nicht-Muttersprache und Translationskultur." *Translation into Non-Mother Tongues*. Eds. Meta Grosman, Mira Kadric, Irena Kovačič and Mary Snell-Hornby. Tübingen: Stauffenburg Verlag, 2000. 5–20. Print.

Reichert, Klaus. "'It is Time': The Buber-Rosenzweig Bible Translation in Context." *The translatability of cultures. Figurations of the space between*. Eds. Sanford Budick and Wolfgang Iser. Stanford: Stanford University Press , 1996. 169–185. Print.

Said. "Briefe, aber an wen." *Eine nicht nur deutsche Literatur*. Eds. Ackermann, Irmgard and Weinrich Harald. München: Piper, 1986. 18–21. Print.

Schleiermacher, Friedrich. "Über die verschiedenen Methoden des Übersetzens." *Das Problem des Übersetzens*. Ed. Hans Joachim Störig. Stuttgart: Henry Goverts Verlag, 1963. 38–70. Print.

Schmidt-Bergmann, Hans Georg. "Von der Gastarbeiterliteratur zu einer neuen deutschen Literatur." *Bitburger Gespräche, Jahrbuch 2010/1*. München: C.H. Beck, 2010. 99–107. Print.

Sengupta, Mehasweta. "Translation, Colonialism and Poetics: Rabindranath Tagore in Two Worlds." *Translation, History and Culture*. Ed. Susan Bassnett and André Lefevere. London: Pinter, 1990. 56–63. Print.

Skiba, Dirk. "Ethnolektale und literalisierte Hybridität." *Migrationsliteratur. Schreibweisen einer interkulturellem Moderne*. Eds Klaus Schenk, Almut Todorow and Milan Tvrdik. Tübingen: Francke Verlag, 2004. 183–204. Print.

Snell Hornby, Mary. "'McLanguage': The identity of English as an Issue in Translation Today." *Translation into Non-Mother Tongues*. Eds. Meta Grosman, Mira Kadric, Irena Kovačič, and Mary Snell-Hornby. Tübingen: Stauffenburg Verlag, 2000. 35–43. Print.

—. *The Turns of Translation Studies*. Amsterdam: John Benjamin, 2006. Print.

Sofronieva, Tzveta. "Unterhaltungen deutscher Eingewanderten." *Feuer, Lebenslust! Erzählungen deutscher Einwanderer.* Ed. Maximilian Dorner. Stuttgart: Klett-Cotta, 2003. Print.

Spivak, Gayatri Chakravorty. "The Politics of Translation." *The Translation Studies Reader.* Ed. Lawrence Venuti. London: Routledge, 2000. 397–414. Print.

Stackelberg von, Jürgen. "Blüte und Niedergang der 'Belle Infidèles.'" *Die literarische Übersetzung.* Ed. Harald Kittel. Berlin: Erich Schmidt Verlag, 1988. 16–29. Print.

Tanzer, Harald. "Deutsche Literatur türkischer Autoren." *Migrationsliteratur. Schreibweisen einer interkulturellen Moderne.* Eds. Klaus Schenk, Almut Todorow, Milan Tvrdik. Tübingen: Francke Verlag, 2004. 301–315. Print.

Tawada, Yoko. *Where Europe Begins.* Trans. Susan Bernofsky and Yumi Selden. New York: New Directions, 2002. Print.

—. "A Conversation with Yoko Tawada." *Community Video.* Stanford University DLCL. 18 Feb. 2009. Web. 27 Jan. 2011.

Three Percent. "Translation Database." *Three Percent: Resource for International Literature at the University of Rochester.* University of Rochester. n.d. Web. 7 Aug. 2010.

Tuschick, Jamal. "Träger von Zukunftsinformationen." *Morgenland. Neueste deutsche Literatur.* Ed. Jamal Tuschick. Frankfurt am Main: Fischer Taschenbuch Verlag, 2000. 283–291. Print.

Tytler, Alexander. *Essay on the Principles of Translation.* New York: Garland Publishing, 1970. Print.

Uzun, Mehmed. "Separation is such a Grief." *Mehmed Uzun.* 22 Oct 2009. Web. 11 Aug. 2010.

Venuti, Lawrence. *The Translator's Invisibility.* London: Routledge, 2008. Print.

Venuti, Lawrence. "Mémoires of Translation." *Exchanges: A Journal of Literary Translation.* The University of Iowa. Spring 2010. Web. 15 Sep. 2011.

Waldmann, Guido. "My Experience of Editing Giovanni Pontiero's Translations." *The Translator's Dialogue.* Eds. Pilar Orero and Juan C. Sager. Amsterdam: John Benjamins, 1997. 95–97. Print.

Winkler-Pöhler, Beate. "Zum Schreiben in fremder Sprache." *Eine nicht nur deutsche Literatur.* Eds. Irmgard Ackermann and Harald Weinrich. München: Piper, 1986. 51–54. Print.

Wischenbart, Rüdiger. "Translation Sells." *Ueber:blick* 2 (2011): 21–22. *Frankfurt Book Fair.* Web. 26 Mar. 2011.

In compiling the present anthology, I was guided by several practical considerations that determined the selection of authors and texts and shaped the overall makeup of this collection. A central requirement for choosing a text was its publication history; to the best of my knowledge, I only included texts that had not been previously published in English translation and that, for the sake of contemporariness, were published within the last ten years, i.e., from 2000 to 2010.

I wanted to present a wide and diverse range of texts and authors with different cultural backgrounds, dispositions and affinities with the German language. As a result, the anthology includes ethnic German writers from non-German speaking cultures, first and second generation migrant writers, writers who publish in more than one language, and writers who live outside the German-language sphere but write and publish in German. For the sake of my own sense of direction and partiality, I included only authors who hail from "East of Germany": Eastern Europe, the Middle East, the Far East. I also included authors who represent the three major German speaking regions: Switzerland, Austria and Germany. I aimed to limit each author's entry to texts of about 3,000 words in length, which, with a couple of exceptions perhaps, I managed to apply fairly consistently.

I set out in the present prose translation to retrace the original text by following its texture and tone, by mapping and documenting its representation. As a non-native translator, my vantage point is the original—from here my writing extends to the translating language. I am less inclined, therefore, to seek out fluent echoes of the original in the receiving language, less responsive to normative conventions of style and idiomatic usage. I am interested instead in articulating the materiality, the ambiguities and the instabilities of the foreign text. The following comments aim to provide a brief illustration of common issues I encountered working with the different texts and of how theoretical considerations discussed in the introduction impacted on my practical approach.

"Mother Tongue," by Emine Özdamar, raises the central question of how a fractured language with its inconsistencies and frictions is retrieved, how the authenticity of nonstandard German can be maintained. In translating the text, I preserved the original form and accent and avoided attempts to rationalize and repair. Tense changes within sentences or punctuation, for instance, are an integral part of the original composition that requires to be carried across in the translating language: "I was in Istanbul in a wooden house, there I met a friend, a communist, he doesn't laugh, I tell him about someone who tells stories from the corner of his mouth, shallow. Communist-friend said, 'Everyone speaks like that.' I said, 'What do you have to do to speak with depth?' He said, '*Kaza gecirmek*, experience life-accidents.'"

In Hertha Müller's essay, the language is fuelled by the distinctive imagery and tonality of the old German dialect she grew up with in the Banat region of Romania. Müller's writing, as I have pointed out in the introduction, is steeped in wayward, tangible expressions and somewhat archaic angles, in dislocated sentence structures. "The tower had the land in its grip, it drew back the ground and the sky, and for all the people in the village in the ink there was only the one tiny, solid place at which they found themselves right now." I sought to retain the awkward, obscure aspects of the orginal and allow for its uncertainties and inconclusiveness to unfold in English: "The frogs and crickets were at their service. At night they said something transparent to the living that was meant to confuse the head."

An exchange with fragmented or raptured language material is characteristic of Ilma Rakusa's writing. "Summer," the author's ramble through Berlin Mitte, plays out in sentence fragments and staccato phrases, in allusions and references that require familiarity not only with the specific locale but its history and structure, its ambience and colour: "The night sky already blue, the chirping subsides. Overarching, the German backdrop. *Mit hinten Linden*, laterally damaged building. The outlook is rumbling inside." I avoided complementing or interpreting the text and, in this particular passage, left the reference to the famous *Unter den Linden* untranslated and italicised, as the original phrase is not readily intelligeable to a German reader.

I also considered it crucial not to alter or polish clichés or awkward and laboured passages. In "Kobra," by Artur Becker (as in all the translations in this volume, to an extent), I preserved the occasional stiff or clumsy expression as an aspect of the text's instability, thereby retaining the original's peculiarity, or, in reference to Benjamin, the author's mode of meaning. Comparably, the tone and rhythmic structure in Dinev's "A Light Above the Head" manifest in laconic, abrupt punch lines: "It was a safe bet. Times were hard. Many would die. Did Plamen want to team up? Plamen wanted." The last verb *wanted* looks misplaced or at least in need of an auxilliary. The verb repetiton is, however, part of the text's use of rhythmic intensification, and to replace it for the sake of fluency (Plamen did) would deprive the sequence of its ambition, its motion.

Another common issue is the differences in German and English punctuation. The writing of Feridun Zaimoglu, for example, whose earlier and more experimental work I briefly discuss in the introduction, required a few minimal interferences. The oral, hip, sardonic quality of his text is expressed in long, uninterrupted speech or thought segments that are held together by commas in defiance, at times, of punctuation rules. The missing breaks or pauses can cause confusion and strain in English. In order not to oversignifiy a familiar feature in the original, I replaced punctuation marks where the flow of the narrative might be obstructed. Overall, I aim to conform to the author's usage of punctuation, layout and rhythmic structures, as in the example of "Mother Tongue" by Özdamar given above or in Banciu's opening paragraph in "Flowers for Mother":

But didn't say if it was important for him.
Or. For whom. And why.

The Gahse text "Short Unstable Locality Guide" features numerous unusual word compositions that I tried to render in English. Words such as "residentity" or "setities" defamiliarise the English reader (in the latter case, for example, the original word *Angessessenheiten* is just as unfamiliar in German), but at the same time the inventive elements in Gahse's inquiries are predisposed to extend to other languages. Common and unproblematic shifts between word classes in German are potentially unsettling in English; where possible, I have followed the author's patterning instead of applying familiar idiomatic usages, a working proposition I implemented throughout this project. In Marica Bodrožić's first story, for example, *Adria-Schönheit* is rendered as "Adria beauty" instead of the more rounded, seamless "beauty from the Adria," and I likewise abstained from replacing the names of places with their English versions, i.e., Wien not Vienna, München not Munich, etc., to allow for their originality and specificity to resurface where it mattered, as, for example, in Gahse's text.

It has to be emphasized that in reference to vocabulary, translations are of course context-dependent and vary according to voice, formality, style, or emphasis. In Mora's "Strange Matter," for instance, I translated the neuter German pronoun "man" as "you" throughout the story, as it's told from the point of view of a young girl, whereas in the more formalistic, distanced writing of Müller, it is always translated as "one." In Tawada's texts, the "you" was more appropriate to the casual voice in "The Apple and the Nose," in contrast to the translation of "one" in the cultural milieu of "Letter Music"; in Banciu's "Flowers for Mother," both forms are used within the same text.

Working on the translation of the present collection of prose texts, I did not set out to foreignize or estrange the translating language for its own sake but compromised with English grammar and style—I do believe, however, that every language has the capacity and disposition to evolve and expand, as well as the scope to accommodate or at least allow for innovative, unconventional and unfamiliar linguistic forms and representations. In this process of language development, literary translation plays a pioneering role.

The Translations

Carmen-Francesca Banciu

BLUMEN FÜR MUTTER
FLOWERS FOR MOTHER

I brought flowers. But Mother wasn't used to flowers. I am not dead yet, she said. I didn't know what to do with the flowers. The fleshy roses appeared obscene all of a sudden. She said: Throw them away. If you can't think of something better.
I couldn't think of anything. As if I was petrified.
You should come, Father had said on the phone. It was important.
But didn't say if it was important for him.
Or. For whom. And why.

I should come at once!
And I had taken the first flight.
Did she want to see me?
And did I want to see her?

A smell of burnt dolls mixed with the scent of chrysanthemums floated in the room.
But chrysanthemums only existed in my head. And the dolls, that happened a long time ago.
I had brought roses for Mother.
Mother was lying in bed. She said I should pray for her. Mother said *pray* as if it was the same as washing hands. I had only been taught to wash hands.

I can't pray. Mother didn't tell me anything about praying. So that I don't rely on anyone. You can only rely on yourself, she said. And I memorized this lesson very well. I memorized this lesson and forgot it again at once.

Can you imagine? I memorized it for good and at the same time I forgot.
Do you know how it is when you know something and you don't?

When you can do something and you can't? Then you feel that you exist. You are. And you are not. And you long for your own being.

You must think I am crazy. I am not crazy. I am and I am not. But is it any different with you?

I am not talking to you. I am talking to myself. To the part of myself who knows. And who can. And to the part of myself who doesn't know. And can't. I am about to learn how these parts can be matched with each other. Reconciled. United.

And what is to come of it? Neither one nor the other? No. A whole being. A being in balance.

And what is balance? Do you know what balance is?

I am not sure either. Although I can feel it some days. I feel my feet. Pressing softly against the asphalt. I notice how my foot is lifting vigorously to position itself again. Like a dance. A chain. Time and again. As if you were floating. But you are not floating. You are walking. You are walking with yourself. No. You are just walking. And you are not. But you feel. I am.

Sometimes you are walking next to yourself. Sometimes with yourself. Turning inward. And sometimes you are just walking.

What does she want to hear from me, the young woman. She sat down at my table. Without asking for permission. We only know each other by sight. She comes to the café every day to read the paper or to look at the people in the café while she endlessly sips at a small mocha. Today she looks agitated. She talks. As if she is driven by something. Without waiting for an answer.

Balance. What is balance? And who is in balance? the young woman says. She doesn't look at me. She looks out of the window. Into the distance. Into a kind of distance where time and place disappear. Balance, she repeats. Is the president of the republic in balance? The pope? The mother of God?

She interrupts herself only briefly and looks into her cup, as if there, deep inside the cup, she has discovered a world. Then she continues. She is in balance. The mother of God. She can balance the pain for the lost son with love. Neutralize it.

She can love the world unconditionally.

And Mother. My mother. Who did she love? Did she love me?
She often said so. Every time I wasn't allowed to do what I wanted
to do. She forbade everything for my sake. Because she was worried
about me. Because she was afraid for me. Because she loved me.
Mother loved Father and me. Yet Father was allowed everything. He
was allowed not to come home at night. Although she worried about
him. Father didn't come home because he worked for our society. For
communism. He always had something to do somewhere. Only at
home he had nothing to do. Because his duties could be better carried
out elsewhere. He came home to please us. Although it wasn't pleas-
ant to have him home and not to have him.
To have him at home always meant to show consideration for him being at home even though he had to be elsewhere.
When do fathers have to be at home?
Fathers never have to be at home.
Because fathers earn money and earning money doesn't happen at
home. But mothers also earn money. And it doesn't happen at home
either. And still they have to be at home.
Mother wasn't at home. And if she was, she wasn't really there. Because
she had to carry out the housework. So that her housewife qualities
were admired. Or at least so that it couldn't be said that she wasn't a
good housewife.
Mother was good at everything. She was even good at being a housewife.
I don't know if she was good at being a mother. But can mothers be
asked such a thing.
Can such a thing be questioned?

Mother was lying in bed. I can see her in my mind as if it was today. Mother was worn out. Squashed by life. Her strength had been
squeezed out of her. I am looking for the right word. To describe what
had happened to Mother, the woman says.

The woman is called Maria-Maria.

She came to Berlin from Bucharest. After the revolution. She came to find out if she could rely on herself.
Throw away everything and start again. From scratch. Make something of nothing. And how can that best be accomplished?
You leave everything behind and go away. Into another world. Where you have to learn everything anew. The language. The way you turn door-knobs. Flush toilets. How you open windows. How you get money from the teller machine. If you have any.

Maria-Maria says: I came because I didn't want to visit Mother's grave. I never wanted to go there. Because Mother isn't at the cemetery. She is somewhere else. I don't know where she is. Sometimes she is around me. Sometimes she is inside me. And sometimes she is gone. Sometimes she is in my fears. I have a lot of fears. They are Mother's fears. But I'm learning to defeat them. I'm learning to drive out Mother.

Mother burned my dolls. So that I don't rely on anyone. As soon as I started school.
My bed was surrounded by dolls. I had my own room from very early on. So that I'd learn to organize my room. That I'd learn to take responsibility for my own space. And my life at the same time. Mother never had time. She had just enough time for me to organize my life. But no time to live it with me. To experience it. Mother didn't experience life. Mother had duties. From morning until evening. And even at night. But she could hardly ever fulfil her night duties. Father was hardly ever at home. Mother performed the duty of headaches. The duty of her daily headaches.
In my memory Mother always had headaches. As if she was born with them. As if headaches and my Mother were one and the same.
I was also familiar with pain. It followed me for a long time. Until I slowly learned to shake it off. To dissolve it. To free myself from it. Mother had taught me to love pain.
I loved my dolls. I could talk to them. I couldn't talk to Mother. Mother never listened. I talked to the dolls, but Mother said don't talk to

yourself. Only mad people do, and your grandmother.
For Mother, Grandmother was the worst example.

The first day at school had been a special day. Not only because of the newly printed books that were waiting for us neatly wrapped on each desk in the classroom.
I had been long familiar with books. I could already read and write and count. Mother had taught me. I had to learn fast. Because Mother had no patience to explain something twice. And certainly no time.

Seven years, Mother said, and you are going to school already. You are a big girl now. You have to rely on yourself. Dolls won't help you with that.
On my first day at school Mother burned my dolls. I was supposed to read. I was supposed to learn. Devote myself to the pursuit of knowledge.
Knowledge was like nourishment for Mother. And yet Mother had condemned the knowledge of others. You should know everything there is.
Not really everything. Mother didn't want me to know about happiness. You can't rely on happiness. If happiness exists at all, Mother said, it comes rarely and vanishes fast. And afterward you fall into the hole it has left behind. And suffocate. And drown. And never get out of it again.
Mother hasn't got out of it either. Mother hasn't found a way out. Although she didn't believe in happiness.
What did Mother believe in?

You should rely on yourself. Reading. Learning. Knowing. Only rely on what you have achieved yourself. On your strength. Your virtues. Mother was virtuous. Now she lay there in bed with her virtues and said: Pray for me.

＄

I visited her in hospital that morning, Maria-Maria said. Father had called. And had said I should come. I was afraid to see Mother. But now Mother could not beat me anymore. And burn my dolls. Now she could not do anything anymore. But lie in bed. With her head on three pillows. And still it wasn't high enough. Rather sitting than lying. Or the water from her lungs would have poured into her throat. And she could have suffocated.

The images one has of suffocation. As a child I believed one could be strangled by tying up one's wrist. Or the waist. There are many forms of strangling. One can be strangled by tying up one's thoughts.

Thoughts are free. No one can control them. It is the only freedom that exists unconditionally. Mother thought it was different. She thought it was her duty to go through my exercise books. To search my pockets and my satchel. She thought a mother was in charge of everything. To drive out daring, undesirable thoughts. All the thoughts that made her anxious.

Most of what I thought made Mother anxious. When Mother became anxious she got a headache.

When Mother had a headache she was unapproachable.

I didn't want to approach her. I avoided her. Most of the time I avoided Mother.

Mother didn't believe in the right to unspoken thoughts. A mother has to know everything. But even to your mother you can't confide everything.

I took care not to confide in Mother. It had been like that for a long time. Since Mother had burned my dolls. And I wasn't allowed to cry. Because at seven you are a big girl already. And go to school. And it isn't proper to cry.

Because something else was expected of me, said Maria-Maria.

She is looking into her cup with the coffee grounds. She is tipping it forth and back. Small autumnal landscapes appear in the cup. Brown and white. Maria-Maria destroys them with her forefinger.

Maria-Maria says: I arrived on the first plane. Mother lay in bed and didn't know that I was coming.

The day appeared painfully red-grey. A day in the life of my mother. A normal day. Yet it was Mother's last day.

She had woken with a restlessness in her throat. The restlessness had grown and spread. It had occupied her throat and had moved to the mouth. The mouth full of pebbles. The restlessness had spread to the lungs and farther into the stomach like a mushroom. A sticky lichen.

I've still got a lot of time. Mother says: Go. Do your things. I don't need you. And if I do, I'll call for you.

Mother did not want me in her dying.
Later Father said that he understood.
The radio played a broadcast of the first school day. It was my first school day. I had written the text myself. Spoken it myself.
But Mother couldn't stand it. Not my voice either.

Mother looks at the flowers. These flowers are withering under my eyes. Mother thinks. I can hear her thoughts. She looks at me and signs with her hand. The words don't come out. Her gaze is black. Mother is a hounded animal. She can only gesture with her hand. Get rid of them. They stink.
I see the words in her eyes. I can read them. Wherever I look I only see Mother's eyes. And in her eyes sits fear. The fear of not being able to see me anymore. And the fear of having to put up with me. To put up with me being here. Now that she wants to go.

Did Mother want to? No, now she had to go.
Now that I was here she had to go. Mother couldn't stand it. She couldn't stand my voice. She couldn't stand anything about me. There-fore she sent me home.

Father had said it was important that I come. But Mother got a fright when I came.

Is it time. Yes, it is time.

She knew it, and she didn't know. She had decided. Or however it is when you die. You always decide somehow. Somewhere inside. At some point you decide. It is a fleeting thought. Like lightning. You let it flare up briefly. Later the head forgets. But the cells don't forget. They prepare themselves for the long road ahead.

Mother's cells had had enough for a long time. I have only known Mother as an old person. For me it's not worth it anymore, she used to say. For her nothing was ever worth it. Only for others. Life should be lived for others. And Mother didn't know anymore why she should live for me. She hadn't been living for Father for a long time. That's not entirely true. She would have preferred to live for Father. But Father lived for others. Or he lived for himself.

Or did he live at all?

And Mother. Had Mother ever lived?

Mother had also lived for society. For our society. For communism. Everyone should live for it, she said. And especially Father said it.

Maria-Maria says, Mother held down air in her stomach. The air she would have needed to breath. She had breathed only shallowly. And it hadn't been enough to be truly alive.

The café is deserted at this time. Even the waitress disappeared in the kitchen. Maria-Maria looked to the window and farther beyond. Into the room of her thoughts. She looks into the room where the mother was lying.

I look at Maria-Maria. I see Maria-Maria with the bunch of flowers in her hand in front of the bed of the mother. The flowers are quivering. Maria-Maria first looks at the flowers. Then she looks around. She wants to make the flowers disappear. She is captured by the eyes of the mother. Captured by the bunch of lead. The bunch is growing bigger and bigger. Maria-Maria is a child with an oversized bunch of flowers at the bedside of the mother.

The mother lies on a catafalque and looks like a hunted animal. And the mother has blue lips. The lips are dry and sticky. The teeth of the mother are dead. Dead-yellow. I see Maria-Maria trembling. And after she leaves the sickroom she throws up in front of the hospital. It erupts from within her. The fear. The disgust. She doesn't know what it is. It is something that ravages her stomach. She calls it a captured boxer. Maria-Maria is sitting opposite me and talks.

 c/s

I stood there with the bunch of flowers in my hands and didn't know what to do with them. I should have hugged Mother. She lay there supported by several pillows. Her lips were blue and dry and stuck to her gums. Her gums were blue-grey-red. The hair on her skull fell in strands and had turned grey all of a sudden. Suddenly she was old. Very old. She was transforming under my very eyes. I saw Great-grandmother underneath her skin. She lay on several pillows. Mother became older and older. Until I couldn't recognise her anymore. Her temples were made from parchment and the skin above the cheek-bones stretched and was about to tear. I was afraid of Great-grand-mother. Who was lying in bed all of a sudden. And said: Go, I'll call for you if I need you. Great-grandmother spoke with Mother's voice.

Mother never needed me. Mother never asked me for anything. She gave orders. Giving orders was Mother's way to communicate with me.
Sometimes Mother ordered: Get me the belt.
And I brought her the belt.
And she beat me with it.
She beat the rage out of her.

I held the flowers in my hands and didn't know what to do with them.
Who had ever given Mother flowers.
I've never given her flowers. Except on Mother's Day. Mother's Day was the 8th of March. It was international. You honoured all the mothers of the world by honouring your own mother.
We honoured our mothers at school. The honoured ones were at their work place. Fulfilled their duties. We sang songs for them. And we re-cited poems. The mothers had ironed our pretty uniforms so that we showed ourselves worthy on stage, honouring them.

Mother never noticed any of it. But the honouring was in the air and perhaps it reached Mother in a mysterious way. But Mother never talked about it.

It was always like this. You honoured the children of the world by celebrating Children's Day. On Children's Day we were also on stage. And sang and recited to honour childhood. Being children. And the children of the world. And felt sorrow for those children who didn't even know that they were children. Because those children had to work. Were exploited. Or had to shoot with a gun. Shoot other people. Never had the opportunity to celebrate childhood as we did.

I've never given Mother flowers. Only on International Women's Day. On the 8th of March. Mother received the flowers symbolically. In fact, comrade teacher, who was also a mother, received them on behalf of all the mothers of the world.

No one has ever given Mother flowers. Father didn't even know that flowers existed. At home we had plastic flowers. Roses that last a lifetime. Which last longer than a lifetime. Which can be passed on as a present.
Vanity, waste of money. And roses. Mother had absolutely nothing to do with it.

A day in the life of my mother. Maria-Maria said. I would have loved to be present at any one day. I would have loved to know what Mother thinks. Who Mother is.
Once we wrote an essay for Mother's Day. Each of us about our own mother. About her role in our society.

Who is my mother?
My mother is the most wonderful mother in the world. My mother is a tractor driver. She works on the collective farm and digs furrows into the soil with her tractor. Then she plants the grain in the furrows with a sowing machine. The seeds sprout and grow. In sum-

mer, Mother returns with the harvester and harvests the grain. From
the grain bread is made. For the world. Mother can also bake bread.
The bread is fresh and tastes good. My mother is the most wonderful
mother in the world.

It wasn't my essay. It was the essay of Dorin. And we all admired him.
Because he received the first prize at school that year. Whoever received the first prize was loved very much by his mother. Because she
was proud. She was proud to show the other mothers on Mother's
Day how well she performed her tasks as mother and how useful she
was for society.
Each mother who was useful to society was a happy mother. We were
told at school. There are only happy mothers in our society.
Mother was useful and yet it was obvious that she didn't belong to
the happy mothers.
In the first years at school I tried hard. I received the first prize. But
Mother's face didn't light up with pride. I hadn't been able to bring
out that warming, all-embracing smile in her.
Mother didn't know the word happiness. It wasn't part of her vocabu-
lary. It wasn't part of her life.
And Father said: We didn't expect anything else from you.

1

Witold Siadek sat on the motorbike and smoked a cigarette. He had been waiting for two hours now and was slowly losing his patience. He wiped the sweat off his forehead, put his hand into his trouser pocket, searched for something that he didn't need.

He was an old fisherman. His wife held it against him that fishing was all he had ever learned in life. But he told her to shut up or else he'd smack her nut. He looked solemn today; tie and shirt and Sunday trousers. Usually he was in rubber boots and had a cap on his head.

When he saw his nephew Janek walking across the schoolyard, he got up, stubbed out the cigarette with his shoe and wiped his moustache with his hand, although it was dry.

Janek Nacktarsch[1] said, "I see you're still riding this old bike without a licence. And where's Mother?"

The man considered him with a cold stare, as if he wanted to give him an order and said, "Let's go already!"

The boy didn't object. He tucked the school certificate under his shirt. For three years he hadn't been home. For three years he hadn't seen his mother. For three years he had served time in school like in a prison. Occasionally he had written home and his mother had sent him parcels, food parcels mainly; once a year he got a new shirt.

Now, riding past familiar places through town, it dawned on him that a new life had begun. He had learned the trade of a mechanic and grown up at last. Now he would work on the farm for a few years. Pity. He had gotten used to life in town. To the white shirt he had always worn to school on Mondays. Monday had been a festive day, and after the third, period roll-call was held in the assembly hall. Every Saturday and Sunday he had gone out drinking beer with his mates. He got terribly drunk, learned to smoke and to love girls.

They rode slowly. Time crawled like a worm and Janek held on to Witold. He had always enjoyed riding on the motorbike with him. The wind whirled around one's body, rushed around one's ears. The

1. lit. "Naked arse."

setting sun was shining through the trees, evening had come.

In Czerwonka they ran out of petrol. The rest of the way they went silently on foot. Witold pushed the bike over the sandy ground. When they came through the forest the first houses of Wilimy appeared. The cows lay in the grass as if thrown there.

"There'll be a storm," Witold said all of a sudden, looking over the paddocks.

The boy didn't reply. He felt a weird emptiness. In the morning he had looked forward to seeing the lake again, the village. But now his tongue was stuck in his throat and he couldn't speak.

All around them it was as loud as on a thoroughfare. It was the greeting of the meadows, the crickets in the fields and the farm dogs. The trees swayed and rustled back and forth, the sky seemed threatening to him and thick like olive oil.

He was tired when they arrived home. A light was lit on the veranda. Witold's wife, a plump woman, sat at the table and played patience. She was barefoot, chicken dirt stuck to her feet.

"Woman, we're back!" Witold shouted.

Janek's aunt jumped up with a smile on her face. She hurried toward them.

"Hang on," she said, "I'll turn on the light. Jesus and Mary, Janek, how much you've grown! Gosh, you've become a real hulk of a man! Come inside, you must be hungry . . ."

"And where is my mother?" Janek Nacktarsch asked.

"Didn't you tell him?" the woman marvelled.

"How?" Witold replied, "you need time for that. And besides, she's your sister."

"Time, time!" she was annoyed. "Janek, Janeczku, come here, put your head on my bosom . . ."

"But why are you crying, Auntie?"

"It happened a week ago," she began to tell him. "You've come one week too late. She's not with us anymore. She's dead."

The boy leaped up: "Dead?" he repeated.

"There's no consolation," Witold said. "Here my boy, drink milk, then it will pass."

"What will pass, damn it!?" Janek shouted and in a brusque tone he added: "Where's her grave? We're going to the cemetery!"

"What cemetery? Janek, you know that the whole family is buried in the garden," the aunt interrupted.

"You didn't bury her next to the SS men, did you? And without waiting for me?" he asked. "How could you put my mother into a box with these two murderers?"

"Which murderers? Which SS men?" Witold wondered. "The earth has long devoured them. There is not a trace left of the bodies. The Russians killed them thirty years ago."

Janek dropped his head. He couldn't get a word out. Again he was seized by this strange emptiness. The tongue stuck to his gums. He felt lonely. He didn't notice when the aunt brought him a cup of hot milk.

Later, as he was lying in bed with his arms crossed behind his head and staring blindly at the ceiling, someone cautiously opened the door and sneaked into his room.

"Janek," the woman whispered, caressing his face and kissing his hand. "Janek, my son, don't worry."

The aunt is a good woman, Janek thought, she milks all the cows by herself, cures eels and drinks vodka like a man, knows about mushrooms and bakes a fabulous potato cake; she also earns money in the nearby holiday park; she cleans the toilets and the bathrooms. Witold had stopped beating her, Janek thought about his aunt, but I won't be drinking with them until I have been in the army.

2

A week later it finally stopped raining. The boy began digging early in the morning. The water had soaked the soil. With each thrust the shovel cut easily into the ground. The mighty oak tree, underneath which it was dark and damp, swallowed the gravestones in its shade. He dug fast without interrupting his work for a single moment. After a short while he got hot, over and again he cast an eye at the tree and considered what to do once he had dug her out. All of a sudden a yell: Witold was herding the cows with a stick and when he caught sight of Janek he threatened him with his fist.

"You're disturbing your mother's peace," he shouted from a distance.

But the boy behaved as if he wouldn't hear a thing. He spat in his hands and thought about a new place for his mother.

"For heaven's sake!" the aunt came rushing out of the house: "What would Kobra say, if he could see you now?"

"He would be happy," the boy hissed. "Behind the shed she'll find peace. That's where I'll bury her. The whole damned garden is full of corpses: bones of soldiers!"

That day the sun burned incredibly, men drank beer in front of the shop, sat on the stones and the women swam in the lake. He was pleased with himself. Now he knew that his mother would never leave him again. He could go behind the shed any time and be alone with her.

The house of the Siadaks was at the edge of the village. It wasn't easy to get to. Like all the other houses it was hidden by conifers. The entire village spread out over several wooded hills, and on one of them stood the house of the Siadaks. From here one had a view over the lake in the valley.

When milking time arrived in the evening, Janek was loafing around the paddock, gazing at the dung heap the horseflies, looking at the lake and the house and the pink sun above. Then he thought that this was all a person needed to be happy.

That evening Kobra returned. He had hardly changed at all. Only his skin seemed even drier and the glasses to have become even heavier. They were black sunglasses, and he didn't take them off even at night. Apparently Kobra had been a priest in the past. He had a wooden hut on an island and a bridge he was very proud of because he had built it himself. He always went away somewhere in winter and couldn't he be expected back before late spring. He went everywhere by moped. The people liked him because he wasn't sullen, like the tourists, for example, or his daughter, who visited him sometimes. The girl often wore short pants and shoes with high heels. She walked like a ballet dancer, showing off her legs and her bust. She lived like a moth. At night she played cards with her father or read novels. For the most part of the day she slept. Yet she still looked tired all the time. Janek thought it was because of all the reading. In his opinion, studying in Gdańsk didn't do her good.

Once, while she was preparing for a new exam, she followed Janek's advice and put the books underneath her pillow before she went to bed. This method proved, however, to be an absolute failure, she woke up with a sore head and neck and had to go for a swim after breakfast to sober up.

And the lake was large with plenty of hideaways: nothing but islands, forest all around with blueberries and chanterelles.

Kobra sold eels with Witold, but most of the time he drove around in the forest, and the aunt was convinced that he visited the wife of the forester.

"How are you?" said Kobra, who suddenly arrived at the Siadaks. "What's happening, Janek, what are you up to?"

"Nothing, only got here a few days ago, but I'll probably stay!"

"He already dug out his mother," the aunt interrupted. "She's behind the shed now, but I've forgiven him . . ."

"And who and what else do you want to transplant?" Kobra asked.

"My name," said Janek.

"Have you gone completely mad?" Witold said. "Are you unhappy here or what?"

"No girl looks at me twice," Janek Nacktarsch defended himself, "once I tell her my name: not to mention marriage."

Kobra laughed.

"Kobra," Janek asked, "will you come to the municipality with me about this tomorrow? "

The man agreed. Eventually, the aunt brought a glass of clear schnapps for everyone. Kobra drank slowly, screwing up his mouth and drove home.

The night was hot. Through the slightly open window gnats and small green flies flew into Janek's room. He wasn't asleep yet. It was a full moon. He was looking through the window when the door opened quietly. He didn't move and waited. It began to smell of soap and shampoo. He guessed it was the aunt. She came up to the bed and dropped her nightgown on the floor. Janek saw her fat breasts, which hung down like a cow's udder. The silence was unbearable. The woman lay down next to him and began to caress his stomach, and then further below. He was afraid.

"Remember," she said quietly, "that I'll screw your head off if you tell anyone what we've done tonight."

And later Janek dreamed how something tried to kill him. It was a light, a stream of yellow-orange light, which looked like a pillar stabbing through the ceiling. The light hit him directly in his heart. He began to sweat terribly, called for help, and when he woke up he began to search for his aunt on the sheet. But she wasn't there. He felt disgusted and quickly wanted to forget everything.

3

It was a late summer evening, the 15th of September. Janek Markowski, as he was now called, walked along the path on the shoreline and staggered back and forth. On the stones in front of the shop he had drunk eight bottles of beer and smashed each bottle amid shouting and cheering against a wall.

The big moment had arrived; he had decided to get married. The Siadeks were in need of labour. He wouldn't hesitate any longer and chose a wife, but not just anyone.

That evening, while Kobra's daughter sat on the bench in front of the house and read a newspaper from last week, Janek opened the front gate with a powerful kick and demolished the lock. Kobra looked out of the window.

"What's the matter with you?" he shouted.

"Kobra," the drunk said, "take off your glasses, I want to see your eyes!"

"I've got snake eyes that can kill. Didn't you know?" Kobra grinned. "Ever heard of an albino?"

"So it's true what they say about you?" the boy asked.

"You want to see them? Think about it, Janek, you are drunk."
Janek scratched his head.

"Rather not, and anyhow, it doesn't interest me, I just want your daughter, I want her to be my wife."

"That's your business," Kobra answered.

At the bridge, a boat floated on a chain. Janek pulled it in and prepared it for the trip. He doused the rowlocks with water so they wouldn't creak.

The girl put the paper aside, went to Janek and sat down in the boat.

"You've got some nerve," she said. "You want me to be your wife? You're just a peasant, a little fool! So, where are we going?"

"We're going where the pepper grows, we're leaving and we'll never come back."

Kobra didn't hear these words. He took off his glasses and his eyes with their red pupils were white as milk. He knew that his daughter didn't love Janek; he himself didn't believe in love. At last he could get a rest from his glasses. He hated them. He put them into his shirt pocket and sat down on the bench where the newspaper rustled and began to read.

It was already late when the boat emerged from the darkness. Kobra had a closer look: No doubt, she was returning on her own, without Janek.

Kobra walked toward his daughter when she got to the bridge. The girl shivered like a beaver and her hair was wet.

"He jumped into the water. He drowned, really drowned!" she repeated in tears. "He just wanted to prove that he loved me, he was such a good swimmer!"

"I know," Kobra said. "I know! He wanted to prove that he loved you! He was drunk! I'll drive to the Siadeks, the police have to be called . . ."

The girl sat crouched up on the bridge and cried. Kobra made the sign of the cross and put on the glasses. It was night outside.

Tito ist tot
Tito is Dead

For days the talk in the village was about nothing else. The television was running hot and Grandfather couldn't comprehend how it was possible that a person who had just died and been put under the earth already could be walking up and down the screen. Whatever transpired in Grandfather's head, whether he banished the appearance of Tito to the world of magic, of angels and the devil, or whether he perceived it as a mystery of the modern world, I'll never be able to find out.

I only know that the flickering pictures irritated him. In particular, those famous love scenes in American movies, which swept over him like an oracular waterfall. A kissing scene on the television screen happened for him as a matter of fact and he railed against the insolence of women who didn't care that he was watching them kissing. Those devilish lips that didn't seem ever to come loose again from each other constituted a desecration in his eyes.

My initial chuckle about Grandfather's ignorance was soon silenced. For his question, what else the pictures were if not truth itself, I didn't have an answer. Could this kissing scene mean anything else? Was it only pretending to be real and not keeping the promise?

On that day, the American kissing scenes had disappeared from the screen. They were replaced by red carnations, by generals and newsreaders dressed in black, by children who learned by heart poems for Mr. Josip and craned their cute faces in front of thousands of cameras. The proud mothers simultaneously cried and cleaned their noses that had become sore from the constant rubbing. The death of the comrade had enveloped them—*all of us*—in deep mourning.

Josip Broz-Tito was dead: the man who hung in my classroom with his huge round glasses and whose picture I had received as a badge at my inauguration as a pioneer, together with the partisan-style cap, the red star and the red kerchief. His piercing look decorated every cobbler's workshop, every ever-so bloody butcher shop, every dusty teacher's room in every god-forsaken mountain village, every shopping centre, every office and every classroom. No one was to forget the glorious battles fought by "our men," who had bravely opposed the enemy and defeated them, not only with their weapons, but with their hearts, fearlessly demanding the death of fascism and the liberation of the people.

Grandfather heard it in the early news and called me into the kitchen. Tito was appearing on all channels. Within only a few hours he had become the single image of the nation; the passe-partout was made up of thin, mourning faces.

The radio also responded to the current events: My favourite programme was cancelled. Instead, there was to be a special feature on Tito's life and work, on a Sunday of all days, the day I listened to my revered *greet-and-request* show of the Dalmatian seafarers and sailors. That afternoon I irrevocably lost out on the beautiful mandolin tunes.

My grandfather watched the television screen mesmerized, with one blind and one seeing eye. Worried, he repeatedly took off his cap, only to put it back on again. Over and over he released a short, almost hissed *tss tss*, shaking his head. Now the devil would ride damned mankind to its knees and everything had been in vain. In vain had he been cooking soup for the soldiers in the Second World War because he thought this would be the last war, at least for the next hundred years. At that time a soldier, whose company my grandfather was assigned to, refused to shoot twenty soldiers who had appeared suddenly out of nowhere. I never understood which side these soldiers were on and never asked because the mere image of their execution was overwhelming and the picture my grandfather described over and again cast a spell on me. The commander had to shoot the prisoners himself in the end, after the cook also refused to get his hands dirty. The objectors couldn't escape this random massacre—it took place in the last days of the war. They had the choice of either being witnesses to the madman's solitary glee or standing at the wall alongside the other twenty men. All those present heard the names of the men sentenced to death. The deranged commander ordered them to step forward in single file and say their names out loud. Before the swiftly fired bullets landed in their thin stomachs and the emaciated bodies fell to the ground like flies, their voices were heard one last time.

Later, one of the rare convictions took place. In court the commander met face-to-face with the company's cook, my grandfather, who recited the names of the twenty dead men as if in a trance. At home he also repeated their names while vaguely gazing into the distance. Only in retrospect have I been able to interpret his restless, wandering gaze and I understood only then why Tito's death, despite all reservations about the inviolable greatness of the marshal, filled him with a real sense of loss. Later still I realized how clearly his body must have sensed the tragedy, because soon another war was to break out and separate not only those who hated one another, but, worse, even those who loved each other. Why was it like that? Because war unites nothing and no one.

In the village I heard that Tito had forced the people to live together and now they would seek revenge. On politics and the enemy and all those who had made life difficult for them. And so I wasn't surprised when I read that after the death of Enver Hodscha the Albanians had first of all cut down the state-owned plum trees and sculptured their revenge irreversibly into their own landscape. Barren grasslands spread out where before tree plantations could be seen from across the border. Now one looked at dull undergrowth, at thick, sawn-off tree trunks—witnesses of a time that wasn't granted survival, the plum trees least of all.

I was a curious child and if grandfather didn't tell me a story I made one up myself. Nothing escaped my imagination. Not even the Russians were safe from me. I had no scruples to hold an apple I had stolen earlier from her garden under the nose of our neighbour Svetlana Rodenska as proof of a Russian visitation, and to tell her about soldiers who had searched the "terrain" at night—a word I had picked up from grandfather—and taken only me into their confidence "in this matter."

In Locarni, a part of our village where only hardened party members lived, the tears ran all the way to the Adria, as told among my patriotic relatives long after Tito's death. The reds loved him very much. Their Tito. At school, Marshal Tito still gazed down on us and on our blue uniforms. Even that day his huge glasses looked as if they would come sliding down and shatter on the smoothly polished tiles. We were assembled to observe five minutes of silence. The entire school gathered in a large dark corridor that connected the ten schoolrooms and even in winter was only sparsely lit. In this corridor we now kept silent. In the silence, my thoughts wandered about and I soon noticed that my displeasure with the Tito pictures on television wasn't shared by the other students. Most of them were serious and some bashfully wiped away tears from their cheeks. An avowed stillness seemed to have crept into their faces, as if they were to blame for Tito's death.

I bowed my head and looked at the white silk socks, which peeked out underneath the skirt of my blue pioneer's uniform. In all the confusion not even observant Matilda had noticed that my socks were new. Not to mention the sailors. I knew that they were out there, tuning their radio knobs somewhere in the deep blue of the sea; that they were waiting for greetings, hoping for songs that would take them back to the harbours of their birth, to the arms of their lover, wife or mother. And what did they have to listen to? The comrade radio announcer reported in a hoarse and harried voice about a statesman who was none anymore because he was lying six feet underground and could no longer hold office.

Even that day I went home as usual and told Grandfather about the decreed time of silence. He listened quietly and didn't respond with a single word. A few days later, as if in passing, he said: "Listen, the people from Loncarni, don't say 'God bless you' to them, they prefer to be greeted with a 'Good day, comrade.'"

Henceforth I was very busy to distinguish people from the various corners of the village and to greet them with the right words. And so the awe-inspiring God, dear Jesus and the good comrade began to whirl around in my head until I created a new, pretty bricolage out of it. Comrade Veljko I greeted with a joyful: "Blessed day, Mister comrade Jesus, how is your beautiful wife from the coast?" Mister Velko had married an Adria beauty, Mrs Marijana, and was mighty proud of his sweetheart. At least that's what the old men in my village were saying.

Comrade Veljko was never unkind to me. But it is probably true that he wasn't of a gentle nature exactly; there are gruff and heartless people in every village. One day I understood why some of the village people had been so angry with him. I overheard the comrade on the road talking harshly with his wife. When she told him, the other side was also in her bosom, I noticed passing by how his face clouded over. That's where she came from after all, Marijana continued, irrespective of his displeasure; in her particular case, her heart was beating on the right and on the left side at the same time.

And Marijana wasn't the only one. There were many whose hearts were beating on both sides. Still, or rather therefore, the houses burned, and in the cellars of those who had fled, books were found that had to be classified as dangerous in view of a world in flames. Nothing got lost at that time, no one was friends with one another, and it was meaningless to show understanding for one's neighbour because he had a fondness for Russian or German literature. The kind of literature he held dear was revealed by his abandoned library. Everyone had become neutral, without history, without biography; curiously enough, a "national memory" was preserved in the process. It was probably due to the eyes of Big Brother because once again they were monitoring events. Even if they belonged to a different master now, it was the usual set of big eyes, he just had a different name.

Old Desanka had gone crazy over all these fires. She was playing billiards with the men in her son's restaurant before they withdrew to the mountains where they stayed for a long time; men, who returned weeks later and didn't know anymore who belonged to whom and why their land hadn't been tilled as usual. One of the returnees, a young man with a penchant for rock music and an atheistic temperament, became a devout Catholic who lived only for the holy host on Sundays. Even if Desanka had not gone crazy, her game would have been the sure sign of a change, and the people in the village would have probably agreed with each other in no time that there was something fundamentally wrong with her, which amounted to the same thing. But as it was, one paid attention to the young and old men who themselves became ever stranger and yelled absurd encouragements to each other and said sentences like let's have a coffee in the mountains or a game of bocce, that would be great. Everyone knew that for months there hadn't been any coffee and that not even the most dyedin-the-wool coastal dweller thought about bocce anymore. Least of all in the mountains, where in peaceful times only hungry wolves encountered one another, and where by now canon fire had scared away even the old howlers, who were as used to wars as to rain in winter. Basically, it was the best time for Desanka to go crazy.

The portraits of Tito finally disappeared and were succeeded by new faces. The men who took his place—there were still plenty of butcher shops and classrooms—had an uncanny resemblance to their predecessor. The knowing gaze above the heads of the people united the new rulers. With their invariable portraits they built themselves a bridge across the world high up on the walls. And the bridge turned out to be a suitable place: from here everything was under control.

People have always told stories. Even now, with the new bridge builders having set foot in the country, it couldn't be any different. In one of those stories it is told that, in the days when coffee was scarce and Desanka had gone crazy, men in the Cabinet of the capital city played football with skulls. These lackeys are the bridge piers of the big-eyed rulers, according to whose wishes entire regions were drowned in blood and who later, without batting an eyelid, sold you the red of death as the colour of peonies.

Grandfather didn't experience them in their element, these new Jacks-of-all-trades. He defied them from the start and never learned their ridiculous names. Whether it was his intention or not, he never got used to them and mispronounced these names to amuse, but unfortunately also, and as a rule rather, to ridicule the restaurant patrons. By the time their banners arrived, Grandfather had died. As painful as his death was, his timing was perfect.

DER KRIEGSHEIMKEHRER
THE WAR RETURNEE

It was silent in the large house at the end of the treeless street. Only an old man and his dog hung around in that wasteland. When a bee was buzzing around the dog's ears or one of the stray cats bared its teeth at him, he tried, breathlessly, to free himself from his chain, ran a few meters and was soon thrown back again. The spiral-shaped chain punched wounds into his neck, and the red-glowing holes lured innumerous, green-shimmering flies, which had only been waiting to set upon the big feast. On these hot summer days the air was filled with a monotonous humming, it vibrated like a high voltage power-line. In the remote parts of the hinterland the wooden poles led to a power line cemetery that looked like a shack. There was no sound. The silence resembled that in the large house, where the old man lived.

Everything here took place quietly and voiceless and nothing reached the world outside. As if for unknown reasons the universe had decided one day to haul this piece of earth behind its back. The old man had no family. He was illiterate. Sometimes he watched the news on television, but he did not understand who or what was talked about, which cities and countries it concerned. He did not even know which continent he lived on. But he still had the scent of war in his nose, smelled death in the putrefied air, sensed it in everything, perceived it everywhere. He heard it from the lips of women who woke him each night. Bloodied, violated bodies, who pointed with their fingers to the mutilations, the deep scars in their skin, inhabited his house at night. Often the women begged him for water from his well because their tongues threatened to stick to their gums. He got up and went into the garden. As if the screams had become shapes, he saw them gathered at the curve of the well and disappearing again once their thirst was quenched. From time to time they returned. The old man always gave them the water they requested. Then he went back to the house, lay down on the creaking bed, closed his eyes and fell asleep.

In the war he had lost an eye. An officer had rammed the barrel of a rifle into the left iris. The eye fluid poured over his cheek reddened from the wind and the inner turmoil. He had refused an order to shoot.

When the war was over, he returned to his village. The story about his eye had already reached the people and he was spoken about as the one-eyed, even before he had arrived.

When the grocery man came by, he hurriedly bought the necessary provisions and asked the salesman to let the fishmonger know to come by in the next days, when he had caught fresh fish. His sister-in-law Rosa brought him tobacco from the market and immediately spread the leaves out in the sun for the moisture to evaporate.

Rosa, or, as he said, Rosa's soul, did not disturb his quietude and he allowed her even to enter the property. His former comrades-in-arms had once made an attempt to talk with him about the eye and the war but he had chased them away, fended them off like horse-flies from his gate. Travelers moved south, to the sea. And no one ever stopped to ask the old man for something or to request a glass of water, as would have been customary in this region, because in summer the faithful, pilgrims from distant villages, were also on the road. They traveled for days on end. The house scared them. Once a whole group walked past the silent house. As if in deterrence, the old man was gripped by an unspeakable rage that day. He threw himself on the vegetating dog. One eye of the dog peeked out from under the hissing stick, and the whitish tongue dug itself behind the sharp, yellow canine teeth. The other eye bled. From a distance already one could see the hollowed, perforated spot where the stick had got hooked.

The man gave the dog a dry piece of meat and examined the wounds, which, lovingly all of sudden, he washed with white linen sheets. The sheets he hung up on a washing line plaited from sturdy grass. The smell of fennel settled on the house and the garden and it seemed to have a calming, almost sleep-inducing effect. In that star-strewn night the one-eyed slept for a few hours on the grass next to his dog.

On the next day a cold wind blew past the houses. A storm was brewing and sent ahead its furrowed hissing, its small warning to the people. The low dark clouds wandered like sneaking warriors across the lonely house, from which not a single sound could be heard, neither before nor after sunrise. In the almond tree hung the body of the dog. His fur was moist and sticky.

The one-eyed hung from the roof beam. His skinny body turned around, describing half arches, over and again around its axis. At first fast, then slower and slower. The storm moved over the land and it is said, in that night women and men, children and angels, deer and stork, trees and flowers were hit by lightning such as had never been seen before.

Ein Licht über dem Kopf
A Light Above the Head

After two years of military service Plamen Svetlev was deaf to orders
but all the more susceptible to rumours of all kinds. He heard that
workers were needed in the Soviet Union, especially in Siberia. He
heard that the work was bloody tough and the weather crap. He heard
that as a woodcutter one could earn as much money in two years as
a Bulgarian teacher earned in ten. Plamen didn't need to hear any
more. He didn't want to become a teacher. He registered and went to
Siberia. Everything he had been told was true. It was tough and crap.
Sometimes the work, sometimes the weather, sometimes both. Two
years later Plamen returned to Bulgaria. He brought with him a red
car model Lada and a blonde Russian named Olga. With the rest of
the money he bought a small apartment. Olga had become pregnant
on the road. It was a long trip after all. His parents were delighted,
his neighbours, who were teachers, envied him. He still invited them
to his wedding.

Plamen began to work as a mechanic in the *Kombinat* for non-fer-
rous metals. He earned good money. He enjoyed life. The car waited
in front of the house, the wife inside the apartment. He cleaned the
car and he loved his wife. Soon she gave birth to a boy. He was cute
and sweet. Olga got a lot of flowers, the boy got a name. Wesselin.

Shortly after his birth the communist system collapsed. The Soviet Union lost its power and disintegrated. The woodcutters returned
without cars and without women. The people became courageous and
rose. From now on the Bulgarian communists were called socialists,
military service was reduced to one and a half years, and all factories
harmful to the environment were closed. The *Kombinat* for non-fer-
rous metals was harmful to the environment. Plamen lost his work
but he had no regrets. In those days one had better things to do. The
whole nation rejoiced. Plamen also rejoiced. It was a nice pastime.

Everyone awaited the arrival of brighter times. But along came inflation instead. Groceries disappeared from the shops, money from

the banks. One could only buy bread and yoghurt, unless one had enough money to get supplies on the black market. Plamen found work as a bookbinder. It earned just enough for bread and yoghurt. He got home very late. The streets were pitch-black because the street lamps had disappeared. They were made from iron. Iron could be sold and bread and yoghurt bought. So it was very dark in town at night. Plamen used to walk in the middle of the road. It was brighter there and more secure. Nevertheless, one night he fell into a hole. It turned out to be a shaft. The lid was missing. It was also made from iron.

Plamen's bones, however, were not. Luckily he only broke his left foot, but he lost his job. He stayed at home with his wife and child. The wife sighed, the child cried. Plamen wanted to sigh and cry both at once, but he didn't. He gazed at his foot in plaster and reflected. There was too much pressure on him. He would have preferred to be without plaster, without wife and without child right now. He considered sending his wife and child to Russia and keeping only the plaster, when his friend Trifon called. He had bought two old, black, Party limousines and intended to use them for funeral services. It was a safe bet. Times were hard. Many would die. Did Plamen want to team up? Plamen wanted.

Despite his plaster, the next day he was sitting behind the wheel. Trifon was right. Many died. But most of them were poor people. For their coffins, a tractor with a trailer or a relative's car with a roof they could be mounted on with ropes or wire was sufficient. The kinsfolk weren't too particular. They'd rather spend their money on bread and yoghurt. Only a few could have afforded a black limousine. Except for the mafiosi, but their corpses were rarely found. Business got worse day by day. The only benefit Plamen enjoyed was a free trip to the cemetery for his parents' coffins. It happened within a week. No sooner had they been buried than Plamen began seriously thinking about a change of job. For quite some time he had noticed that the number of taxis had increased enormously. Even his neighbour, the teacher, drove a taxi. And what was he driving? A hearse. The dead have only one destination, the living several. Some take many rides, others only one, the last. For some, time is of the essence, for others only Judgement Day. So it was more sensible to transport the living than the dead. Plamen pulled out of the business, bought a bottle of schnapps and visited his neighbour. He found out that he needed a concession, a car and a taximeter. They would spare him a few problems in this line of work.

He had a car, he bought the concession, and he had the taximeter set up by a versatile student of pedagogy in such a way that inflation couldn't harm his business. Plamen had received a miraculous device. It was ahead of all exchange-rate fluctuations. In Plamen's taxi you paid the fares of tomorrow. As soon as you entered his car, you were in the future. At last he had found his calling. He took people to the future, and everyone wanted to be there.

Things looked up again for Plamen Svetlev. A smile beamed on his face and a sign beamed from the roof of his car. "TAXI," it said. It was a sign of hope for all those who were frightened of the darkness in the streets. Because many things happened there that could strike terror into people. But along came Plamen with the little light on his roof. A rescue for the desperate. One only had to wave him and he offered safety and a future. Whoever can provide in times of need does well and Plamen Svetlev did well. He cleaned his car again, loved his wife, and bought toys for his child from the black market. Occasionally he even loaned money to his friend Trifon, who, after a few failed major business deals, sold popcorn and fake trademark watches in front of his house. Actually, he rented his house to a Greek shoe dealer and lived with his wife and two children in the empty garage. Trifon did not want to drive taxis. He wanted to try something different. And so Plamen lent him money occasionally.

For a year now his car had had the little light on the roof and his family was fed, his wife was loved, his child healthy, and on his parents' grave stood two crosses of white marble. Taxi driving was a blessed occupation.

One night two cheerful young men who wanted to go to Assenovgrad got into his taxi. Assenovgrad wasn't far, only twenty kilometres away, still Plamen pointed out that they also had to pay the return fare because most likely he would have to return empty. They agreed. He drove. They told jokes. He laughed. They offered him a sip of schnapps, he laughingly had to decline. He could already see the lights of the town when they politely asked him to stop. He did. Then he felt a blow to his head and he saw lights again, but those lights were of a town he didn't know. Something cracked and Plamen passed out. When he came round he was lying in a field next to the road to Assenowgrad and had the feeling that his head housed all the crickets of the region. His head wasn't that big. How could so many crickets find room in there? He couldn't explain it. He only heard them chirping. His hearing could not be trusted, so he looked around. The car, the money, the wedding ring and even the gold chain, a recent present from Olga for their second wedding anniversary, were missing. There were many stars and a big round moon in the sky, but they weren't his. He was left with only his shirt, trousers, shoes and a strong headache. His wife and his child were far away, Assenovgrad was closer. He went there. An hour later, Plamen arrived at a police station and frightened the dozing policewoman. "I want my car, I want my wife!" he shouted. Not all of his wishes came true. But his head was stitched twelve times by a young, not altogether sober doctor, and at least he was driven home. At the sight of his shaven head Olga felt sick.

Again it didn't look good for the Svetlevs. Although Plamen's wound healed and his hair grew back, his car did not return. The little light over his head was gone. Their days became black, only the bread and the yoghurt on their table were white. Soon the streets were also white. Winter had come and Plamen still didn't have work.

One day he came home very late. His stomach was empty. It was dark in the flat because he hadn't paid the electricity bill. And it was cold because he couldn't pay the heating bill either.

"The child had nothing to eat today," a voice said somewhere in the dark.

"I know," he said.

"I've sold my jewelry already. There's nothing left," said the darkness

"I know," he said and looked at his feet. Snow was still sticking to them and it seemed to him as if they were in plaster.

"We used to be happy once," Olga said after a while.

"I know," he said and walked over to her.

"You need a car, and things will pick up." The telephone interrupted them. It had been paid and it could ring even in the dark. Trifon was calling.

"My children haven't eaten today," he began.

"I know," Plamen said.

"The Greek hasn't paid the rent for half a year and has disappeared," Trifon told him.

"Asshole," Plamen decided.

"You're not doing much better, I guess. But I've got an idea . . . and I've found a buyer already," Trifon changed the topic.

Plamen was silent.

"Do you have a crowbar?" Trifon asked. He had an idea and a buyer, Plamen had a crowbar. "Then get it and come over fast," Trifon suggested.

Plamen took it and went. Trifon had a buyer for the icon of the Virgin Mary in the church of the same name. It was old. It had performed many a miracle already, helped a lot of people. Now it was Trifon's and Plamen's turn.

It was three o'clock in the morning when the door finally gave way. In the church it was even colder and darker than in Plamen's apartment. They switched on a torch. The icon smiled at them willingly. It was still and quiet. Plamen relaxed. At last he had the opportunity to research the mysteries of a church, and he went searching. He returned with a silver crown on his head. In the meantime, Trifon had woken the icon from its slumber and was about to wrap it into the piece of cloth he had cut from his curtain at home. Suddenly a shadow appeared and began to scream. Trifon held the icon in his hands, Plamen held the crowbar. So he struck out with it. The shadow fell and fused with the darkness. They ran away. A few streets later Plamen stopped. "The crickets," he said, surprised. "What crickets? Now, in winter?" Trifon dragged him on. "But he's got them in his head! I have to go back. He's got them in his head for sure," he said, handed the crown to Trifon and ran back.

With the help of God and in rustic Russian style the head of Father

Illarion was stiched eighteen times that same night. He came round and the first thing he wanted to know was which circle of hell he was in. Father Ilarion after all was a sensible man.

Plamen, on the other hand, who had admitted the Father to the hospital, was in a well-heated police office, where two sweaty police officers asked him the same question over and again. "I was on my own. I threw away the loot. I don't know where it is," he repeated. Now and again Plamen was beaten with the city's telephone directory. The city's name was Plovdiv and it was the second largest city in Bulgaria. More and more people had a fixed-line telephone by now. It was not just a large but also a practical book. Even Plamen's name and address could be found in it. Trifon's name could have also been found in it, but he was in Austria. And besides, no one was looking for him.

A month later the icon of the Virgin Mother fulfilled her overdue miracle. She surfaced unexpectedly from the luggage of a German antique dealer. Even he was most astonished and overwhelmed by this miracle. There is still some mystery happening in this world.

What happened to Plamen was of a less sacral nature. He ended up in the prison of Haskovo where he was to enjoy a lenient five-year sentence. His wife wrote him a single letter and came to visit only once, to ask for a divorce.

"The boy is still small. It will be better for him. It will be better for all of us. I want to be happy again," she told him.

"I know," he answered and consented to the divorce.

Olga took Wesselin and went to Russia. Now Plamen had lost his car, his wife, his child and his freedom. He cleaned his cell and wanted to sigh and cry all at once. Only his cellmate wanted to love him, but this made Plamen even sadder because he didn't love him back.

Eventually Plamen got used to his new life. He was tall, and that helped. Since he was a good worker, the guards respected him. He decided to get a tattoo. He had a good look at the tattoos of his fellow inmates to choose a suitable one for himself. It was to be discreet and original. The spot where it ought to be was just as important to him. His cellmate had a spider on his penis. But spiders disgusted Plamen. Women's names he found banal, the most interesting sayings too long. On the dick of a pimp he finally found what he was look-

ing for. The word "taxi." With this he could identify. He sent for the
tattooist immediately. His soul found peace and the four letters only
hurt for a week.

The days dragged on hard and slow as if shackled to a chain. Plamen fulfilled his duties, listened to the stories of his fellow prisoners,
gazed frequently through the bars up to the sky, which appeared blu-
er to him now, and thought about his life, which seemed far away.

Sometimes he remembered his wife, his child and his car. His
wife's name was Olga and she had shapely, warm breasts. His child's
name was Wesselin and he was sweet and cute. His car was red and
had a little light on its roof. There had been light in his life back then,
now it was missing, even a little one. After two years Plamen Svetlev
was given three days' parole due to good behaviour. He had experienced more in these two years than his teacher had in ten. It was
Christmas. Plamen had neither family nor friends to go to. He only
had the address of an Armenian watchmaker and forger of passports.
So he went to see him. He was led into a room full of ticking clocks.
He paid and sat down in an armchair that also seemed to be ticking.
The Armenian took his photograph and disappeared into an adjoin-
ing room. Plamen stayed and waited. He listened to the clocks and it
was as if he could hear the passing of every single second of the three
years he still had to serve. Three days later Plamen Svetlev's return was
awaited with apprehension in the prison of Haskovo. The apprehension grew, but a Plamen Svetlev did not return. He could not have returned, as such, because there was no Plamen Svetlev anymore. From
now on his name was Pyros Putakis, he was born in Thessaloniki and
enjoyed, as a free citizen of the European Union, an untroubled journey to Vienna. In Vienna he met Trifon who still had the same name,
had remained a Bulgarian, but had a new life nevertheless. He had a
small apartment, lived on his own and earned an honest living as a taxi
driver. Trifon still owed Plamen half of the miracle the icon of Virgin
Mary had performed back then. He owed him a new life. Trifon was
a grateful man. He showed Plamen his apartment, his kitchen and his
bed. They sat at his table, drank his schnapps and looked out of his
window. He talked about his life and about his work. Plamen, on the
other hand, said very little and had only his new passport to show,

his new name and the four letters, which had hurt him for a week. It wasn't much, but it was enough to start a new life.

A month later Plamen had the same friends, two months later the same boss as Trifon. He had the job again that he had always loved. In his hands a wheel, under his feet four even bigger ones, above his head a little yellow light. Wrapped in his luck he sat as if in a cocoon. He drove a taxi again. Someone looked for a street and he showed him. Someone mentioned a road and he knew it. Someone inquired about the travel time and he told him. Time and space had an exact price. Plamen knew it and his knowledge was rewarded. He was again what he once used to be. Only the streets weren't as dark anymore but saturated with light. Only he didn't have a wife and child anymore. Only his name wasn't Plamen Svetlev anymore.

A year later he rented his own apartment and made the acquaintance of loneliness. Some days it treated him harshly. On such days he could eat only bread and yoghurt and leave the apartment. He got into the car, drove to the Prater, chose a woman, who, like himself, knew exactly the price of time and space, let her get in the car, parked in an underground car park, switched off the light on the roof, felt how the letters in his pants got bigger and more distinct and let their light go out on the backseat. He never got out of the car. He was only happy in his car. And so time passed. He worked a lot, paid his bills on time, and when loneliness treated him badly again, he satisfied his hunger with bread and yoghurt and his desire in underground car parks.

One day a coffeehouse was searched by the police. Incidentally Plamen was sitting inside. He had just ordered a Melange. They didn't find what they were looking for so everyone's papers were checked. Plamen was a citizen of the European Union, which obliged him to remain calm. They looked at his Greek passport and his Bulgarian smile for a while. One of them they didn't trust. Plamen was taken away, his Melange was left behind.

The streets were wide and bright, in the car it was cramped and dark. It was the first time that he sat in a car and he felt the presence of a much bigger light above his head and still wasn't happy. Plamen's passport turned out to be false. Now the police wanted to know to whom his smile belonged. He was interrogated by three police officers. One of the officers had been to Rhodos on holiday, apparently he had even got a Greek woman pregnant. He asked Plamen something in Greek. Plamen remained silent. He had never been in Greece on holiday and the only woman he had got pregnant was a Russian.

"No can speak, hey? Only know 'ouzo' and 'tsatziki'?" the officer said.

"Where are you from, you wog?" the second one asked.

Plamen was thinking. He heard the ticking of many clocks. They had already counted the life of Pyros Putakis and kept ticking. They interfered with his thinking. Because he hadn't answered a single question he was forced to undress. The sight of his tattoo amused the police officers.

"A word at last! And look where he's hidden it!" the first one delighted.

"We'll find the others as well," the second one said.

"He's done time for sure," the third one announced himself for the first time.

"That's what I call a pedigree cabby. Just remains to be seen what you're driving at, pansy," the first one said.

"Take a seat and you'll find out. I guarantee a comfortable ride. You'll most certainly enjoy it," Plamen said with impeccable pronunciation and the nonchalant courtesy only a person who has lived in Vienna for four years is capable of. Then he felt the blows. They beat him with the Vienna telephone directory. It had three volumes. Vienna is a big city with a lot of companies and a lot of people. Plamen was beaten in all of their names. He thought it was amusing that so many names were required to find a single one, his own. He started laughing, instead of fending off the blows. Shortly after he saw the lights. They were the lights of a city he didn't know.

Kleine instabile Ortskunde
Short Unstable Locality Guide

A precaution against all possible misunderstandings: the word migration is not connected with *Migros*.[1] Migration means wandering. But *Migros* is also a kind of foreign word, and one foreign word soon leads to another, although in this case the confusion is revealing, as it is always the foreigners who migrate. Migraine.

Emigrants and immigrants are foreigners. If someone suddenly wanders from one place to another and doesn't return to the original place for a while (the question, of course, is how long is a while), he will gradually look disfigured, and this is what one perceives as foreign.

For my part, I repeatedly moved to new places over several years, always in-between, to Wien, Hamburg, München, back to Wien again; now I am in Switzerland for a while, but I will move on perhaps, so I am here only in-between, and this is something different from setting out to change life forever and not having to move on ever again. I am a transmigrant, I have the world-famous Alps in front of me every day now, probably not forever. I do everything daily, but not forever, and my surroundings show it.

The surroundings always show it. It is also noticeable when someone has been away from his home for a long time, when he begins to lose his habits or has already lost and forgotten them.

Habit is an important word in the context of migration. Truly sedentary residents have habits that can be observed by everyone wandering by. There are numerous short-term wanderers who are on the move solely to observe the habits of sedentary residents; on their travels they look out for habits and notice that the habits of the locals depend on the landscape. Mountain dwellers, for example, have good lungs and they ski; whoever lives at a lake takes walks along the shore;

1. A Swiss supermarket chain.

and people in big cities take buses and the underground to cope better with the streets.

At any rate, landscapes and habits are connected, even today, and such connections are recognized most easily in people who reside permanently at a place. To observe migrants and to draw conclusions from these observations is less straightforward, and this difference makes it problematic to talk about wanderers and permanent residents.

On the other hand, sedentary residents are really interesting because there are so few of them left, everything and everyone is in motion, is on the move, as often as they please. But it wouldn't be right to call those who like to be on the move migrants.

Everyone now is on the move from time to time, therefore the sedentary residents, the indigenous residents, are in demand. A sedentary resident has lived at a place for a long time, so long in fact, that a residentity has emerged.

The other lost his face. At first he smiled a lot and how he ought to smile he'd been taught at home; then he emigrated, he was young and he relearned. He acquired a serious facial expression, with which, after his second emigration, he didn't get anywhere though. In this second, new environment he didn't get anywhere, not ever. He believed to understand the people and responded—he was there, present—but for the others he remained incomprehensible, as if he hadn't arrived yet, and so he lost his face for a second time.

Losing one's face is rather symptomatic of wanderings. At a new place no glance in the mirror helps, nothing helps, no one is obliging, one's facial features are unfamiliar, at first to others, gradually even to oneself.

Unless the arrival is an already well-known personality; in that case, the facial features have long imprinted themselves on everyone, long before he has arrived, and then the foreigner is foreign in a very good sense. Someone can also be foreign in an exceedingly good sense, that is, not really foreign but known, known as a foreigner, and what is known beforehand almost everyone will be interested in beforehand.

To wander or to reside. In the past, residing meant something like wandering, namely, to search (for whatever sustenance could be found). The word could change further and expand, new possibilities would be: to reside oneself in, to reside upon, to re-side oneself with an area, to pre-reside a country, to get resided with others.

Getting resided, would however, have to be practised by all participants at the same time. Of course someone has always resided and settled longer in a given place than whoever came later—what else?—but over time, one could reside together, whereby the new and the old wanderers and the new and the old settlers shouldn't concern themselves too much with time. If an individual or a family or several families have been sitting at a place for just a few weeks, and other people come wandering by to sit there also, there will hardly be difficulties (unless there is no inch of space left for the newcomers). But with time, the older residents get distinct residentities and setities, and they have the feeling that a place belongs to them and not to others.

In the past I enjoyed talking about emi- and immigrants, I immediately thought of Beckett, Oscar Wilde, Gertrude Stein, Gombrowicz, Ödön von Horváth and other authors who didn't live in, and not necessarily for, their country, and I believed they were good for that very reason, which I still believe.

In his diary Gombrowicz wrote that as soon as one mentioned an Englishman, a Frenchman or a German, a whole person became visible without further description; as an Englishman or German he could even appear in a novel and would be recognizable for the reader. With the lesser-known countries it was different; people from those countries had to be accurately characterized first (otherwise they had no face). —To observe migrants or to have them appear in a novel is considerably harder. What migrants!

Beautiful foreigners, they belong to every country and belong to themselves, I thought. Accordingly, I was happy with my own story, I thought it was good to be able to belong to Wien and to Hamburg and to many cities more.

I know a Frenchwoman (a woman from a well-known country), she has been living in Germany for decades but can't settle down quietly; in this case it is *her* who doesn't want to forget where she comes from, perhaps she wouldn't even want to in a hundred years' time. Or in three hundred years. Some live in other countries for hundreds of years and remain who they were before. Even though one hundred years are a century (according to Gertrude Stein), and a hundred years couldn't pass without changes. One hundred years are three generations and it is unfortunate if one hundred years don't change anything. It is unfortunate if after one hundred years the sitters or the newcomers still resist. Time isn't a trifle. No one is able to claim that it doesn't exist.

Or is there someone who thinks there was only one single decisive time, the past, an undetermined early past, in which a particular place had been decided for everyone? And now an old order had to be re-established, a clean-up was needed and all the Germans, together with all the Romance and Slavic tribes, would wander back to where they once came from; the Spaniards, and of course the English as well, had to be brought back from America, until they could or had to return to their ancestral place in Indogermania, the Hungarians had to move with the Finns over and across the Ural to the Altai mountains, where, although that relationship has not been entirely established yet, they would meet up with the Japanese, and there the Inuit would already be waiting. Everyone would be, as they originally had been, happily together, as if they had only been transmigrants in the long meantime. But are they ethnically together? Or will they be forced together and back according to linguistic criteria. Who has to return to which time?

It will always be revealing to know where someone has come from originally. Even with words it is like that, the past is interesting. To know where someone comes from will always be exciting, but also where he is going. Why does someone go further and further away from his original place, what is drawing him where? Where does he want to belong so urgently and why?

I could move to Odessa or Montreal now and what would happen then? If I had always wanted to move to Montreal or Madrid, wanted! Where then would I belong?

PELIKAN
PELICAN

He jumped out of a car that had stopped only briefly, then he ran as fast as he could. He was about thirty, tall, not too tall, and visibly pleased with himself. While he was running, he liked himself for about three hundred meters, then he turned into a side street and disappeared. Shortly beforehand, the lights in the house opposite had come on and a naked man appeared in the window, younger than the former, hungry, it showed, an agreeable sight so long as the hungry one remained quiet. He looked at the street below, surely no one would discover him from down there. For days a drunk has been standing next to our entrance, holding his bottles sleepily in his hand, drinking with half-closed eyelids. He saw neither him nor me. Then Joe, his head lowered, approached the entrance and rang the bell. He walked up the stairs. When he entered, he put his head on my shoulders.

Joe is a pelican; others thought he was a stork, but he is not, despite his adaptability, that's how he can be misunderstood. Pelicans wake up two times a year and are almost always melancholic in the meantime; I say this because he would be even more desperate if someone called him despondent. In reality he is despondent, then he overcomes himself, flies up for a moment, makes loud noises in the air, lands soon after and says he would love to look bulky. He isn't hungry. He doesn't like it when someone talks about how small his appetite is. As soon as he notices that he isn't bothered by hunger, he gets afraid I might reproach him for something and he immediately puts his head on my shoulder and then I put my arms around his head. It's all right, it's bearable, I manage for hours. But after twenty-four hours, at the very most, I start arguing, gradually to begin with, declaring at first that I'm not a pelican, then saying quietly that I get melancholic if I have to act melancholically, whereupon he drops both large wings in a way I haven't ever seen other birds do, as if he wanted to shake out his wings, like a dusty or dirty blanket, his head twitching; I go under cover; he's had enough of me and my impatience, he says.

This time his feathers were sticky with grease, he couldn't clean them because he had injured his beak two days ago, he continued shaking his wings slowly, but it didn't help, and there was absolutely no reason to be happy. He didn't have fleas, I assured him, and his feet were okay, but we would have to trim his claws, that is, I'd have to trim them for him because he couldn't look down to his feet, from time immemorial he hadn't been able to look at himself in a mirror, me neither, because there are no more mirrors, and there is also no more glass. Almost all window-panes have been made anti-reflective, others have wooden or iron shutters. This surely was the reason for the man in the opposite building to stand in the open window because the presence of others has the effect of a mirror, and if someone doesn't have this presence other possibilities have to be found. I, for instance, have only seen myself in fragments, never seen my back; sometimes I see my legs, suddenly discover a run in a stocking. I have runs in my stockings, therefore I am.

We should eat something, Joe said, and dragged himself into the kitchen. On the street three policemen ran in the direction of the railway station with flashing torchlights in their hands. Joe said it didn't interest him, his sore throat was meters long, and all he had left was the thought of food; but he neither wanted to say what pelicans like, nor have I ever seen what he's eating, what he's devouring, if he is on his own, once he's gone. He doesn't fly when he leaves the apartment, he walks down the stairs and slams the gate shut.

Now he was talking, as he got downstairs, with the drunk, who didn't, however, answer him, that much I could gather. At least there are lights again in the streets, sloppy lights are wobbling, a few cars are on the road. Someone just stopped and threw books from a car onto the footpath, bundled stacks of paper, crumpled envelopes, and there were probably also letters among them.

SAGT NICHTS
SAY NOTHING

An eternity until all words are tidied up! Tidied up so that each
word—one has to imagine the volume—that each single word can
show itself from all sides, so that everyone can see where it comes
from, what it wants to say, what it doesn't say simply because it cannot
say it, or because its tongue has been torn out, no, that's too graph-
ic, because its meaning has been fractured; one day its meaning was
interrupted, that's how it is with some words, with others, however,
it was never interrupted. Some words can shine forever without being troubled a great deal. The word eye, for example, is really old, a
beautiful word, it stays put, remains undamaged, therefore one can
see with the eyes. And apart from the eyes, the whole body, almost the
whole body, has kept well so far, arms, legs and mouth are called what
they are called, whereas the legs would have to tell their curious story (they won't, big silence regarding the past); yet wine, the word that
is, used to be foreign, then settled down, into the language, and tulip
and rose also sit in the midst of it, not symbolically, but they actually
positioned themselves so that they don't appear foreign. Even though
they were foreign at first. Curiously enough, many plant names are
concealed, so to speak, and why exactly they have been provided with
foreign words would require someone's explanation. As if plants of
all things, flowers, had something to hide, roses, lilies, gladiolas, as if
even more had to be kept hidden about them than about one's body.
As far as I'm concerned, I'd like to see all words in such a way that I
know where they belong, as I don't just talk out of myself, but with
them, with their help, I have to say.

This is what I wanted to talk about yesterday, there was a small reading, I had prepared a text and before the reading the listeners arrived
who had agreed to listen to the text, or rather to be presented with
words they themselves also often throw around. Missiles (*Gere*) fly
around, fly constantly, one could bundle them, bring them to the

market, the weekly market, throw them around there—people do it. Or is the word bazaar better than market? Do we live in a bazaar economy? Go to super bazaars to prop up the economy? But to return to the word throwing: chucking, stirring, dashing used to be synonymous once, unbelievable. And to return to the listeners: many of them knew each other, there were embraces and kisses, and they said, you're looking good, you're really looking good, you're looking very good, or they said, and you're looking so good today, or you're looking good today, better, how good you're looking today, you're much younger today, they shoved on, past each other and a few steps farther they said, you're looking good, today you're looking very good indeed.

EIN ZARTER BAMBUSSPROSS
A TENDER BAMBOO SHOOT

Early one morning, Bai walks on the road from Yanting to Santai. She has shouldered her satchel and tied a colourfully checked scarf around her head, just as if she wanted to go to the market and then to school.

But there is no market today and her school lies in the opposite direction. Two peasants walk toward Bai. They carry firewood on their shoulders. Bai pulls the kerchief down to her eyes and changes to the other side of the road.

It is January and freezing cold. Everyone is preparing at home for the spring festival. There is hardly anyone on the road. A strong wind blows into Bai's face. As if it wants to drive her back. She is squatting down. She can't walk anymore.

In the afternoon two bicycle riders give her a lift, one after the other. When it is getting dark, she arrives in Santai.

After losing her way three times, she finally finds the street where her aunt lives. But there is no light coming through the gaps in the door-frame. She knocks for a long time.

In the light of the only street lamp she can see a man slowly approaching.

"Are you looking for old woman Wei?" the man asks.

"She is my aunt," Bai says. She can hear her voice trembling.

"She left a few days ago. She's gone on a pilgrimage to Putuo Mountain."

Bai is freezing. "When is she——?"

"Don't know," the man cuts her short, already moving on.

In the residential blocks for the teaching staff of the middle school Bai inquires about her former teacher Li. He moved to Santai two years ago. But no one has ever heard of him.

Bai withdraws again into the dark of the night. She doesn't know anyone else here. She looks around for a place to sleep. In the school building she finds a corner that seems suitable. But the naked concrete floor is so cold that after a few minutes she leaves the place and the school again, shivering.

Midnight is approaching. It is getting colder. Bai can hardly put a foot in front of the other. Suddenly the smell of five-fragrance-eggs fills the air and draws her irresistibly closer. She doesn't have to walk far before she finds the stall where the eggs are sold. She buys two and gulps them down greedily. She is the only customer. The street and the city centre are completely deserted.

"Are you from the country?" the old egg seller asks. Her voice is hoarse.

Bai can't turn her eyes from the steaming egg pot. All she still owns is a two-yuan note and she wants to keep it. Yet she doesn't move from her spot.

"You're not from here." The woman calmly places the eggs in a large Guo.

"I'm from Yanting," Bai says quietly.

The woman eyes her bluntly. "I bet you're still at school."

Bai doesn't answer.

"You need a place to stay girl! You look like a frozen strawberry! You better come with us. You can't stay out here in the cold!"

"Let's go little tiger," she calls into a dark corner, "nap's over!"

A child drags himself from the dark into the light, a seven- or eight-year-old boy with dishevelled hair and a dirty face. He rubs his eyes sleepily.

"That's my son. A good-for-nothing! All he's good at is eating me out of house and home." She turns to the child. "What are you waiting for, you little devil?!"

The boy takes a stool in each hand and trots behind his mother, who has started to move her four-wheeled stall. Bai follows them.

The woman's house consists of a single room, where it is hardly warmer than outside. The walls are slanted, as if about to collapse at any moment. From the ceiling, above which the roof is arching, the scurrying and scratching of a hundred mice's feet can be heard.

The woman brings hot soy milk, dried tofu, peanuts and half a bottle of liquor. Little tiger is squatting on the floor and rips the feathers from a dead sparrow.

"Drink, my little girl! It's good against the cold!" She places a bowl in front of Bai, half-full with liquor.

Bai smiles shyly. "I think it's too strong for me."

The old woman laughs. "When I was your age I couldn't down that stuff either. In those days everyone called me 'Lily.' The young lads came from who knows where just to see me." She casts a glance at the child and screws up her face. "Those times are gone. Today I consider myself lucky if I scrape by. This small, crummy crab here gobbles faster than I can fork out." She jabs her chopsticks at the boy's head. Impassively, he continues eating. The whole time his eyes are fixed on Bai who greedily gulps down the meal. All of a sudden he throws away his chopsticks and pulls so hard at Bai's ponytail that she falls backward onto the bed. He laughs and Bai notices that he's got almost no teeth left.

"Looks as if he likes you," his mother comments dryly. Then, enraged: "But all he's got in his head is nonsense! He spoils everything!" Abruptly she tears hard at his ear. He screams and tries to hide behind Bai.

"Stop your bawling right now!" the old woman barks at him. In an instant he falls silent. "I'll break your neck one day, with your constant blubbering!" One of the chopsticks cracks between her fingers and snaps.

"What else do I have to do until you get it? It doesn't come any easier than today! I distract the salesman, and you snatch two, three dried squid. Then you clear off. But you're not even capable of that!" She takes her bowl and throws the soy milk in his face. Little tiger cries.

Bai wants to leave. She summons her last strength, picks herself up and tries to reach the door. Confused, little tiger follows her.

"Hey, hey, what's going on here? Here's the bed, you two! What do you want out there? There're only ghosts who have no home prowling around now!"

Bai holds on to the doorframe. "I'm used to cold wind."

"I can see that from your skin," the old woman says mockingly. "And I bet you're also used to men who loiter about at this hour waiting for tender meat. Only last week they found another dead girl in the people's park. No one knew her. And now, off to bed!"

Bai returns to the table, grabs the bowl with alcohol in it and knocks it back.

Bai wakes up because her head is bumping against something. Her whole body seems to be in motion. She wants to reach out for little tiger but can't move her hands. Again she receives a bump. And suddenly she realises that she is in a sack being carried by someone. The horror overwhelming her at that moment makes her pass out. Her mouth wants to scream. But she's gagged. She wants to wake up. But she's awake. She feels how urine is running out of her, warming her thighs. Her head is heavy. Her heart is racing. She is gasping for breath. Slowly she remembers drinking the rice wine before going to sleep. She doesn't know that a sedative had been mixed into the soy milk the egg woman offered her.

"Quiet, my sweetheart, quiet. You won't be harmed." It is a soft male voice. At the same time a hand feels her back. Suddenly two fingers stab between her shoulder blades. It's as if she's hit by two electric rods. She loses consciousness.

When Bai comes to again she feels a smooth, cold surface underneath her. She's still stuck in the sack. It smells of blood and urine. Her whole body is itching. She tries to rub against the coarse sack linen but to no avail.

Then she can hear a door being opened and a man saying: "Wait, I'll have to look at her!"

Another male voice answers: "You'll be pleased. A most tender bamboo shoot. You're really lucky." He gives out an obscene laugh. "Start lighting the fire between your legs and warm up your flower!" He laughs again and then the voices disappear. Shortly after, the door slams shut. A noise can be heard as if a wooden latch is being pulled shut. Again footsteps are approaching. Someone begins to busy himself with the string with which the sack is tied up. Light appears in front of Bai's eyes. A man stands before her and grins. His teeth are protruding. He bends down to her, and again she smells the blood. She has to cough. The man spits into his hands and rubs them together. "You're my wife now, kitten."

The man pulls aside a curtain and goes into another room. Bai can see that it is full of hides hung up for drying, and small skinned animals. They must be rabbits or cats. The sight of the raw meat frightens her. The man returns. He's got a long knife in his hand. Bai is staring at the shimmering blade in disbelief. The man comes over to her. Bai can hear herself screaming very loudly. The man holds Bai's head down on the floor with one hand, with the other he brings the blade to her face and performs a short, skilled move. Blood is oozing from a cut on Bai's cheek next to her left ear, it is pouring into her nose, mouth and eyes.

The man gets up. "My name is Tu. You are Yuer."

Bai's screaming turns into sobbing.

Tu goes into the next room and returns with a handful of ashes. He spreads it on Bai's wound.

"Your hair has to go," Tu says. Once again he's got the knife in his hand.

Bai starts screaming again. But Tu is already kneeling on her with one leg, pulling her long, dishevelled ponytail with his left hand, moving a sliver flash past her face with the right, and a moment later he holds Bai's hair in his hand. Again he disappears behind the curtain.

After a while he comes back with a bowl that gives off a smell of ginger and chives. He places it on the table and unties Bai.

"Eat the liver soup. You need strength."

Bai tries to get up. But her legs don't want to carry her. She touches the wound on her cheek with her hands and gropes for her cut hair. She feels nothing. Her fingers are all numb.

Tu drags her to a bed, covers her with a dirty blanket and feeds her. Bai avoids looking at him.

Then Tu gets up. "I have to slaughter two pigs today. After that I'll see the head of the village and register our marriage. Don't try to run away. With the cut on your cheek everyone will know that you belong to me. They will send you back to me."

He steps outside and locks the door behind him.

Das Liebespaar, die Polizisten und der Einbrecherkönig
The Lovers, the Police and the Burglar King

The night lies black and heavy above West Lake. No breeze ruffles the vast expanse of water. The branches of the willow trees on the shore droop motionlessly. It is very still.

Only two solitary figures stroll across the long dam that divides the lake. Occasionally they come to a sudden halt, one of them gestures with the hand or the arm to underline what he is talking about, then they keep walking. As soon as they have reached the shore on one side they turn around and walk in the opposite direction.

When Su San and Ma Sai arrived here a few hours ago, the lakeside promenade and the dam were still full of walkers. The two students hardly noticed that they had gradually disappeared, that it had become ever more deserted around them. And it didn't much interest them either. They don't need anyone else on this balmy night. Like all people about to fall in love they are content with themselves. They are talking about their school days, about their universities and the plans they have for the summer holidays. They talk incessantly, and yet, it is what they *don't* say but feel all the more strongly that is the true reason for their midnight stroll, for continuing to walk from the eastern shore to the western and from the western back again. This night, if it were up to them, would never end.

For the two policeman Kang Zhengqi and Dong Penglin, who are driving up the dam in their police van, however, the night shift is almost over and done with. During a routine patrol they have caught a big fish in their nets, the burglar king You Long, who has always boasted that no policeman in the world could catch him. Unfortunately, the arrest hadn't come off as smoothly as the two custodians of the law would have wished. You Long resisted, and Kang in particular shows it. There are still traces of dried blood under his nose, and his left eye is swollen shut, which dampens his mood despite the unusual success. Among his colleagues he is not only known to be reckless and combat skilled but also brutal and ruthless, and the black eye will, at least behind his back, most certainly provoke some ridicule and derisive remarks.

"You're going to regret this," Kang shouts to the back, to the built-in cell, "I'll knock your teeth out, I swear."

You Long doesn't answer.

"I'll squash your balls to a pulp," Kang keeps threatening, "I'm going to crush you like a louse!"

"I have to take a leak," his colleague says.

"Me too," Kang answers.

"Then pull over, man!"

But Kang doesn't make any move to take his foot of the accelerator. "Have a look," he says, "what have we got over there?"

When Su San and Ma Sai hear the engine noise, they stop at the side of the dam and look toward the approaching headlights. The van jolts past them and they recognize the writing on the side panel in four cake-sized characters, "special vehicle for public safety."

To the surprise of the students, the car comes to a halt after thirty, forty meters. Two policemen get out and while the young couple instinctively slow down their pace, the men in uniform line up next to each other at the side of the dam and piss into the lake. In the silence of the night the splashing can be clearly heard.

"Actually I don't want to continue in this direction," Su San whispers.

"But we can't stop now," Ma Sai replies. "How would it look!"

"Let's turn around."

"Just like that, right here?"

"Why not?"

"They'll get suspicious."

"Let them! We haven't done anything."

"All right," Ma Sai says. But his facial expression remains sceptical.

They've hardly taken two or three steps in the opposite direction, when they hear a loud voice in a commanding tone behind them: "Hey, you two over there, stop!"

"I told you," Ma Sai whispers.

"There's nothing they can do," Su San whispers back.

A few moments later the two men in uniform stand in front of the couple and eye them suspiciously.

"Where are you off to in the middle of the night?"

"Nowhere," Ma Sai replies calmly. "We're just going for a walk."

"I see, that's how it's called nowadays." Kang, the bigger of the two policemen, looks at the young people sardonically. "Well then, let's see your ID!"

Neither Ma Sai nor Su San have their papers on them.

"It just keeps getting better," Kang says grimly. "Sexual acts in public and not even able to identify yourselves." And turning to the girl: "Did he do it to you already, or was he just about to do it to you?"

"Stop insulting my fellow student!" Ma Sai's voice sounds unmistakably angry. "I've already told you that we're going for a walk. No more and no less!"

"What do you know," Kang answers viciously, "the son of a bitch is getting cheeky." With a quick move, he grabs the young man between the legs. "I bet you've still got a hard-on!"

Ma cries out in pain.

"Hey, what's all that about, kiddie! You're howling at a policeman? Did you get what he just said, brother Dong?"

"I think he said filthy pig."

"So I heard correctly. Pretty cheeky, that boy. Or is he allowed to do that?" Kang's voice sounds ostensibly harmless.

"I'd say he's not," Dang replies friendly.

"That's exactly how I see it."

In a flash Kang pulls up his right knee and thrusts it into Ma Sai's groin. The student screams again, doubles over and at the same moment receives a hook to the chin. He falls over, groaning.

Now Su San, who has been standing there frozen in terror, lets out a piercing scream.

"Oh dear, now our little whore starts singing. Probably her mating call—or what do you think brother Dong?"

"Absolutely," Dong confirmed, "this wimp here was only her appetizer at most."

"Run, Su San!" comes a weak gurgle from Ma Sai's half-open

mouth. He lies writhing on the side of the road. A pool of blood has formed in front of his face.

"Stop whining, son of a bitch!" Kang kicks the student in the ribs.

"Run!" Ma Sai gasps one more time. His voice is hardly audible.

Su San takes half a step toward him but then surprisingly turns around and runs away.

The two policemen exchange a brief glance, Kang nods in the direction of the disappearing girl and they're off running after her. One can see from their movements that they're in good shape, even the bullish Kang has a astonishingly strong start. The distance between them and the girl is dwindling fast. When they've almost reached her, when Kang is stretching out an arm to grab her, something unexpected happens: The student ups the tempo, hardly noticeable, yet enough to avoid the outstretched arm of the policeman. He begins to stumble, swears, gets his balance back, panting to his colleague to move his ass a bit faster, they have to get the girl, but as hard as they try, they can't get hold of Su San running in front of them. Had they known that they were dealing with the university champion in the 4,000-meters event, they probably would have abandoned their efforts earlier. But the young woman succeeds in luring them on for another few hundred meters. She runs just fast enough for the policemen to believe that they still have a chance to get her. She hopes that her friend will be able to use this opportunity in the meantime and run away despite his injuries.

When Kang and Dong eventually return worn out, frustrated and seething with anger to their car in which they intend to take up again the pursuit of the girl, they have to realize that someone else has used the time of their absence: the master burglar. The cell door of the van is wide open; there is no trace of You Long anywhere. Kang is in a rage and has to restrain himself so as not to beat up his colleague.

"You didn't tie him up properly, you gigantic arsehole!"

"Of course I've tied him up properly!"

"And how did he get out of there, hah?!"

"How should I know! Perhaps the son of a bitch had a file on him that he got out with!"

Kang leaps into the car and switches on the headlights. They immerse the dam in a glistening light, first in one, then in the other direction, and then the lake on both sides of the dam, but there's no trace of the escapee. Only the student still lies moaning at the water's edge, the body doubled up, face down, exactly as he was lying when the policemen took up the pursuit of his girlfriend. The only thing that has changed is the pool of blood around his head. It's become much bigger.

Kang gets out of the car, walks over to the young man and looks at him for a few moments. Then he walks back again, turns around after a few steps, draws his gun and fires three shots at the student. Two of them hit his back, at the height of the shoulder blades, one hits the back of the head. Ma Sai's body rears up and then remains motionless on the ground.

Dong lunges at his colleague. "Are you insane! You've killed him!"

Kang puts his gun back into the holster. "Is it my fault if he tries to bolt with this criminal? Am I supposed to stand by and cheer them on? They were swimming over there and I aimed a few shots at them. I don't even know if I hit one of them."

Dong bends down to the lifeless body.

Kang steps up to him. "What's there to look at? He is dead! Done, finished. Come on, into the water with him!"

They grab his legs and shoulders and throw him into the lake. Then they get back into the car and drive off.

The body of the student is found early in the morning by a fisherman. His girlfriend, her parents and his own parents press charges of grievous bodily harm and murder. They are rejected. The police officers have given completely different statements about what happened that night. Their conduct had been impeccable, the plaintiffs are assured.

Both families turn to the press. But only a small, regional paper dares to print their version of events. On the day the article is published, the editorial office's phone doesn't stop ringing. A large number of callers report harassment and abuse they have personally suffered at the hand of the police. The authorities act promptly. The editor in chief is summoned before the cultural department of the city administration and transferred on the same day. In the next edition of the same paper a large article is published, praising the tireless and heroic efforts of the security forces in their daily struggle to maintain public law and order.

A year later all media report that one of the most wanted burglars in the country and notorious boss of a crime syndicate, the almost legendary You Long, has finally been caught by the police. They were able to arrest another dozen mafiosi together with him.

Kang Zhengqi, who particularly distinguished himself in the large-scale operation, is going to be promoted forthwith. He is now deputy-superintendent of the criminal investigation department in the West Lake district.

DER ZEITLUPENSCHREI
THE SLOW-MOTION SCREAM

The slow-motion scream occurs at a family celebration. Thirty, forty people, many children, good food. The scream squeezes right into the middle of it. A terrible, protracted and miserable scream. From an unknown throat, it has forced its way through the thick brick walls of the house, the porch and hallway, past the summer-cold oven, through the French doors and has penetrated the living room where people are sitting and celebrating. It reoccurs, piercingly, harrowingly, heartrendingly, and rises slowly but steadily, an awful suffering, full of mortal fear and despair.

The pausing takes place in slow motion. Also the lifting of the head. The freezing of a smile on the lips, the sweeping of a strand of hair from the face while turning around on the heels, the running to the front door and the noise of adult steps in the back. Shreds of words as if in cotton-wool. Above the head, a big hand slowly grabs the door handle, pushes it down for an eternity and opens the door. In a spin the celebrating cluster of people swells into the midday sun. The eyes of children follow the street. It describes a curve in front of the house, running up the small hill. Just as one has to get off the bicycle sometimes and push because it is so steep, the gaze now pushes up the hill.

On top, enthroned, a camel. It is kneeling. Men have arched its long neck backward. Two of them are pushing its jaws against its flank. The others are holding the large animal tied up with many ropes on the ground. The camel is screaming. It knows it is going to die. The camel is all alone.

Everyone is watching how a man with a gigantic knife, a sabre almost, cuts, precisely and expertly, rhythmically, forcefully, the long neck of the camel enthroned on the hill in the sun, until the artery is opened.

They catch the blood in a bowl, which is large and battered, made of silver-white tin. The blood spills over. The camel is still screaming. Men and women stand in the street, look on, talk and get bored, make jokes, scold children who play catch, and carry babies on their arms. They scratch their crotches and under their breasts. They spit to the side and light cigarettes. They shift weight from one heel to the other and chase away a fly.

Later a voice grins through the room. He whom it belongs to bends over from behind the back of the chair and places his arms to the left and right of the plate on the table. From above he looks at his child and holds, pierced on a fork, a piece of steaming lamb in front of its mouth.

"Eat, darling," the voice says coaxingly, "eat the yummy camel meat," and gurgles, greatly amused, a throaty laugh.

The horror then takes place in slow motion. Also the lowering of the head. The cramping of fingers around the hard timber of the armrest and the closing of eyes and mouth. The sound of a voice like cotton-wool in the background. A large hand slowly grabs the chin from behind the head and pulls it around for an eternity. Everyone is watching how the father with a huge fork, a rake almost, stuffs, precisely and expertly, rhythmically, forcefully, meat down the child's throat. They collect the breathlessness, the nausea and the fear in a wave of shrieking laughter while slapping their thighs. Women, men, sit at the table and stand around in the room. They look on, talk and get bored, make jokes, scold the dog who's whining from the garden for bones, and hold babies in their arms. They scratch their crotches and under their breasts. They eat dessert and light cigarettes. The shift weight from one heel to the other and chase away a fly.

Sediment

He is back again. In all his glory. Glowing, glistening, irresistible. He is back again and has startled me, as usual. He doesn't announce himself. He comes and goes as he pleases. Today he caught up with me on the Weidendammer Brücke. Behind me, the rush-hour traffic is roaring along Friedrichstraße. Next to me my bicycle leans against the cast-iron railing. Between the Tränenpalast and the old Brecht-Theater I gaze into the setting sun, sparklingly and dazzlingly mirrored in the Spree. There he is, on the water, big, still and insurmountable. The Damâwand. The mountain. The crown of Teheran. He is on the water, rising out of it to his almost six-thousand-meter height, spreading left and right above the banks of the Spree, settling on streets and houses, and his white-covered head is glowing stronger than the evening sun in Berlin.

My throat is hoarse. I am used to this. First a shortness of breath, then a lump in my throat. I know it will ease if I remain calm and don't doubt what I see. I've tried all kinds of things. Simple things, like turning around or driving off, more elaborate ones, like taking various narcotic substances. But in vain. Once he is here, the Damâwand, he's got his reason. Then he won't be chased away, then he stays where he is and as long as he likes. Anyhow, it's a foolish proposition. To chase away a mountain, to scare it off, to banish the mountain of mountains, how childish.

So, I exhale thoroughly, wait for a fraction of a second, inhale again and look at the overwhelming rock face that has surfaced so unexpectedly in my small, rugged Berlin. The stillness of the Damâwand can be felt all the way down here, and the brown-blue shimmer of his creased, rough-cracked flanks is descending on the centre of my aged, new home. The ochre-coloured village at his foot is dozing in the evening sun although I know that in reality it doesn't exist anymore. It has been swallowed by the city. It might have become the old centre of a new district although it is more likely that it has been levelled to the ground and disappeared. But not its residents, who are poor and without influence. Yes, that's probably how it is. The village would have made way for new multi-storey houses built from cheap concrete, which, like the fin de siècle buildings in Berlin before the turn of the century, were occupied to dry the mortar. Occupied by those, who had lived there before in mud huts and narrow houses of handmade bricks, snuggled up against the rock.

Like music, the car horn concert of the Teheran traffic surges at my ears. The Schiffbauerdamm is festooned with coloured lights, it must be a holiday and it makes my mouth water, when I discover the men next to their small kerosene stoves, who, squatting at the roadside, sell *Labu*—beetroot boiled in saltwater.

At the slopes of the Damâwand in the north of Teheran, the Spree burbles below my feet and one of the punks who have set up camp in front of the Tränenpalast wants to scrounge cigarettes. But I can't give her any, I say, as I don't smoke anymore. She doesn't believe me and insists on at least one. I ask whether she can see the mountain. She can see an old bitch, she replies, exactly where I am standing, whistles to her dog and leaves.

I turn again to the highest of the high. Smoking wouldn't be such a bad idea. I would inhale deeply and then send a long grey stripe of silver into the air. Into the air in front of me, in front of my face. A stripe of silvery smoke that would obscure my vision and hide my presence, hide it from the mountain. Only for seconds of course, for fractions of seconds. Anyway, it would be a foolish proposition. To hide from the mountain, from the mountain of mountains, wanting to scram, to dodge, to slip away.

Absentmindedly I search my jacket pockets for a forgotten pack of cigarettes, but too much time has gone by since I gave up smoking. I still remember the moment clearly. We sat on the steps of a small shop that stood empty like most of the flats in the old dilapidated house. We, Mira and I that is. She smoked cigarettes without filters that smelled like pipe tobacco and brought stories with her. I was responsible for a six-pack of cheap beer and a stack of newspapers against the cold from underneath. At that time I had already switched to a light brand and incurred Mira's mockery each evening. From the end of

March until the beginning of October we sat on the steps until long after midnight, drank three beers each and got lost in what she talked about. In dreams of the future or stories from the past. But they had one thing in common: They all took place in Berlin, in Mira's Berlin, a city I didn't know, its streets lined with prisons, children's homes and asylums. Their most prominent inhabitants were poor whores, rich whores, children and dogs. It was full of politics, heaps of politics. From below, as Mira stressed.

We didn't talk about my Berlin. It didn't interest Mira and I could understand her because my Berlin was blurred. It wasn't clearly visible, it was persistently elusive and remained nebulous somehow. It resembled me: reclusive, a little lost, ugly, contrary and scarred.

On one of these evenings we journeyed to the Söthstraße correctional centre where women, with their backs bent, manufactured wooden clothes-pegs. Mira told the story of a passionate love affair that had taken its course here only to end a few years later, in Italy, as dramatically as it had begun. Completely immersed in her story I repeatedly stubbed out my thirty-seventh cigarette of the evening, and when I finally dropped the butt I couldn't breath anymore. I gasped for air and made squeaking, groaning noises, thought in panic that life couldn't end so suddenly, so unexpectedly, and in such ignoble fashion and heard, through the rising roar in my ears, a voice that kept saying vehemently: "Breathe out! You have to breathe out!" It was Mira who repeated this command over and over, at the same time pulling my arms above my head—a fag in the corner of her mouth. I haven't smoked ever since.

Once I told Mira about the Damâwand. He was right there in our inner court yard. I considered briefly, pulled myself together at last and asked her whether she could see him.

"Who?" she wanted to know.

"The mountain," I said faintly, "over there."

We sat on the window-sill of our dump, fourth floor *Altbau*, and looked down below. It was late summer or early autumn, golden remains of sun rays were hanging over the inner court yard, a few stretched out spider webs, attached to invisible ends that seemed to span from nowhere in front of us, and a smell full of earth, despite all the city around us. The Damâwand was right in front of us. In order to see his snow-covered peak I had to tilt my head back, all the way to my neck. I was happy about his closeness and thought about my father and how he had explained geological formations to me on an excursion to the mountain. He told me about animals that had lived there hundreds of thousands of years ago. Had lived under water because we were walking on sediment rock. On the floor of a primordial ocean, pushed to the earth's surface by gigantic forces—ammonites, trilobites, animals of prehistory with academic names, buried deeply in stone.

"Nope, can't see your mountain," Mira said after a glance at the inner courtyard.

Then I told her about him. How he had turned up on the plane and I was afraid the machine couldn't carry the weight. We, the passengers, the stewardesses, the seats and the small oval windows shimmered through the Damâwand, like the ivy and the façade of the front house now, while underneath, still and unnoticed, my Teheran disappeared. I also told Mira how the mountain had emerged in Berlin at school. In the sports class of Herr Katzing and while cleaning in Frau Malikowski's flat. Always somewhere else, actually.

"And now he's in the inner court yard. Has been here for quite some time. Almost two weeks, I think."

Mira was silent. Then she swung her legs across the window-sill, took a beer can from our newest purchase, a fridge, our pride and joy because it hadn't cost anything and always guaranteed a cold Pils, and sat down next to me again. A hiss whizzed through the kitchen when she pulled the aluminium ring with a practiced finger. As with every beer, Mira drank also this one with relish and appreciation. She watched the inner courtyard attentively for a while.

"Still can't see your mountain," she said and dangled her legs.

I nodded and we kept silent. Then Mira pointed to the silhouette of Herr Börne outlined against the frosted window of his kitchen. He had it installed because he knew that Mira and I, if we weren't sitting on the steps, were lounging about up here, looking into his kitch-

en; which recently had been adorned with a shower cabin. Obviously, the new views thus afforded went too far for Herr Börne and so,
with the help of the blind glass, he had wound back our optical radi-
us to an acceptable level. Mira pointed with her can to Herr Börne's
glass shadow shining through, said that it reminded her of Max, and
began a new story.

With Herr Börne's shadow in front of my eyes, I relinquish the
search for the cigarette and take my hand out of my pocket. Next to
me something is scraping on the pavement. A donkey is standing at
my bicycle. Never before has the mountain gone so far. Focused, I
breathe out and in and out and notice with relief that the little boy
sitting on the donkey is blond and in the company of a colourfully
dressed, well-nourished man decked out with a bell-tipped fool's cap.
He is tossing a small, rattling box with coins back and forth. The trio
is collecting donations for a circus performing in Schöneberg. I need
my money for myself, shake my head and think that the child ought
to be in bed. The thought extends a reproachful look to the unknown
man, which he doesn't understand. The little grey donkey snorts quietly and I could bet that he grins as he looks up at me. In my thoughts
I tell him that I also have to go home now. The donkey nods content-
edly. I grab my bicycle and turn around to wave at the Damâwand.

But he has disappeared, like so many times before. And the good
old Spree is swashing and burbling as if nothing, absolutely nothing
had happened.

Terézia Mora

SELTSAME MATERIE
STRANGE MATTER

Don't you tell anyone how it happened. And don't say anything else about here either.

My brother is worried. We are fertilizing the garden with the content of the latrine. It is too late for it, the new year has begun, the heavy dung from the latrine won't be rotten come spring. Still: we agreed on it last night and began early today when it was still dark. My brother shovels the dung into the wheelbarrow, then I push it into the garden, then I dig up the furrow, then my brother shovels the dung into it, then I cover it up again. As I'm not answering him, we work silently. My hair is still at least five centimetres long in some parts. It is bobbing up and down in the wind, as if it was spring already, as if the fluff of the poplars was sticking to my scalp.

My hair was cut on Sunday. At an unnoticed moment, after we had put Mother into the ambulance and the yard was full of women from the neighbourhood and I had returned on my own with Florian the Gypsy, Father set it alight. And then he screamed in the arms of the men who held and pushed him into the dirt of the chicken yard. In pain. I myself felt none. Aunt Ella was standing next to me and smothered the fire in my hair with the corners of her headscarf. Only one half was burned. From there the hair fell on the ground, like the hair of corn, and some strands were, strangely, not burned at the ends but higher up.

Aunt Ella gave us twenty eggs. They're not worth much, she says. The winter is too warm, that's not good, says Aunt Ella. Not for animals and not for plants and not for people. They become too weak and some of them go crazy, and some die—like our father and our mother. But I, alive and healthy, fertilize the field with my brother, and I hold my head into the balmy wind that carries the smell of our dung to the neighbours, as it carries to us the bitter smell of their burning wood and the ferrets that Attila Hornák keeps on his veranda. We should also keep some, my brother says, we'd make a lot of money.

After the fertilizing I wash my brother's hair and then myself in the washbasin with the monogram. My brother is sitting close by with a towel on his head and is watching me. We always wear our under-clothes when we wash ourselves. Then my brother puts the hat he inherited from Grandfather on his wet hair and slips into his old winter coat. While we are walking to the bus stop at the highway, the wings of his coat flap in the wind like in the movies. My brother has milk-white skin and a dainty figure. Some say he is an imbecile, but that's not true.

We avoid the tractor road and wade through the fields. Elements. It comes to my mind here, while we are walking. Elements.

The elements in Mendeleev's periodic table that my brother, still at primary school, learned by heart. The table hung above my bed because I had to learn it. But my brother didn't learn the complete names, like hydrogen, helium and so forth, only the symbols as they were written: H, He, Li, Be, B, C ... Sometimes he sang them—without melody, but rhythmically—to himself. Ha-He-Li-Be-BeCe-NeO-Fe-Ne. He told our aunts, who eyed him suspiciously from under their headscarves, that it was the language of science, the cos-monauts above us were talking like this—and he pointed to the sky. Our aunts with the headscarves now looked at me, and in a serious tone I said to my brother: Na-MgAl-SiP! When our aunts had left, my brother laughed and said: Au-Hage-Tele-Pe, Bi-Po? I told him he shouldn't talk like that anymore or he'd be taken for an imbecile.

Later I got a five at school because when asked I could only sing the periodic table: Ha-He-Li-Be. The class laughed like crazy for a long time. You should go and see a doctor, the lot of you, the teacher said.

You could have a wig made from it, said Aunt Magdala. We are look-ing at the yellow heap that is lying in the yard. I can only think of us-ing it to seal the dripping water pipe. I shrug my shoulders. We bury the hair in the garden.

No one will believe you. Because, my brother says. The fields we are wading through are muddy. Elementary. From Mother I've learned always to take a second pair of shoes with me when going to town so that I can walk there with clean footwear. And now I'm carrying brown and blue shoes for my brother and myself in my backpack. My brother says I'd better say that I come from the castle.

As a child I was often in the old castle, and although I was afraid of the bats, which get tangled in your hair, I even climbed to the attic and walked up and down behind the backs of statues.

Aunt Ella believes that our golden-blond hair was an inheritance from the counts, that I should have a look at the portrait of countess Maria. There were many golden-blond housemaids who looked the spitting image of their mistresses, says Aunt Ella. They had names like Creszenz, Leonie or Amaryllis. Before the Russians came and parked their tractors on the white marble of the *Sala Terrena*, the maids had taken their due share of the inheritance from the castle. We also have a washbasin with a monogram: F.N.E. Someone else has the matching jug, we don't know who.

Now they want to reopen the castle again, for the tourists, and they are picking up furniture, carpets and porcelain everywhere. Aunt Ella says they'll be also searching our place for the missing items. She has a Venetian mirror in her bedroom that she always covers with a black cloth. When they come, my brother says, I'll bury the washbasin in the yard.

Even now I often dream about the castle. I walk through hazy, empty rooms and colourful laboratories. Until I can go no farther, all of a sudden. Stairs disappear or doors can only be opened by a crack, which I can peek but not get through. Once, in a dream, the whole castle shrank around me, and if I hadn't escaped through a tiny window, getting plenty of scrapes and scratches, it would have crushed me. You're stupid, my brother says, you always wake up beforehand. My brother is often right. But not this time. Nobody I know has dreams like I have.

A teacher once told me that I had a lisp and then he showed me how the *S* is pronounced: with the tongue behind the teeth. But he also said: This *A* you won't get rid of for the rest of your life. I tell my brother it would be useless to say I'm from somewhere else. They'd hear where I was from anyhow.

You can see the highway from far away. You can see the buses of the people who have left an hour before us, yet sometimes you can't even see your own bus. You never know when it's the right time to set off. Sometimes, for inexplicable reasons, the bus simply doesn't arrive. No one informs us and we don't know where to ask about the disappearing buses. It could well be, my brother says, that they have actually disappeared on this long, straight road and no one noticed because no one asked about them. Sometimes the bus drives past us although we are standing on the side of road. It could well be, my brother says, that we become invisible from time to time.

When we're sitting in the bus at last, he counts loudly, with every door opening, how many invisible people might have boarded the bus. And he asks: How long have they been standing there?

In town they tar right to the tree trunk. The roots bulge the pavement, you have to keep an eye on your feet all the time or you trip like in the forest. We're walking in brown and blue shoes. My brother wears a hat and I wear a cap. It is raining on our necks. It is raining softly, in long silent lines, like in dreams I'll be having later about home. I'll be dreaming about this walk in the rain so many times that I don't know anymore whether we actually exist now, whether we're actually walking here, or whether it's a dream I'll be having later.

We are taking a detour across the square where a photographer has displayed a picture of our cousin Marta in the shop window. For two months now. She is right in the middle. My brother says she is not pretty at all. Cousin Marta looks like a doll. Our golden-blond hair curled like the locks of angels, our blue eyes, in her face, round like marbles. I am the only one in the family whose cheekbones have slipped so high that I have slit eyes, like a Mongolian. My brother and I, we look very much alike. And yet he is handsome and I am not. You look like little angels, says Aunt Magdala. We both take after our father. No one would compare our father with an angel.

Our father has many children. My brother and I have many siblings we don't know. But we recognize them when we run into each other. And they recognize us. We are bald-headed babies. Later we grow golden-blond hair that our aunts and mothers press into cast-iron curlers. Sometimes they burn red blisters on our necks with the curlers. Strangers stop in front of us, admire our doll clothes and marble eyes, and we don't say what our names are. We squeeze the chocolate bars in our fists to brown lumps the tin foil sticks to, and the fairy-tale pictures, which sometimes hide underneath.

At the hospital we don't take off our hat and cap. Mother doesn't notice that I haven't got any hair left. She is admiring my brother, how elegant he looks in Grandfather's coat. Small squares of paper bandages lie underneath her bed; it seems they are smeared with black car grease. I don't know what's wrong with our mother. I don't even know if she is our mother. She is so thin, so black-haired. How can it be that she recognizes us at all as her own? We haven't brought our mother anything to eat, no compote, no cake. We should have bought flowers at least, my brother says when we are outside again. At the hospital gate a peasant woman sells chrysanthemums. As if it were a cemetery.

You can't leave, my brother says to me. If you leave, I'll become like Kelemen with his bicycle. Kelemen with his Uschanka and half an eye can't ride a bicycle, but you never see him without his rusty frame. He pushes it along next to him, through the furrows in the fields, across the highway, past dead cats, dogs, roes and partridges, like old women with their sticks, who don't want to admit that they need one. Kelemen is a field guard, and he is always drunk. And he shows the bicycle tourists, who roll past here in summer, where the ripe fruit can be found in early August, because on their own, the bicycle tourists wouldn't find it. The field guard Kelemen feels attached to bicycles, pats them and winks with his eye at the tourists, most of whom can only speak foreign. But my brother won't be like Kelemen. My brother is handsome. The girls will look after him. He'll have eight children. Golden-blond.

If they ask me I will tell them that I come from nowhere and don't know anyone. I exist just like that. I can sing. I sing the arias of Sarastro from the *Magic Flute*. And I have learned several male parts. And since I was eleven, I have known the names of the chickens of the great Romulus. Domitian was a bad emperor.

If you leave, you'll become a hooker, my brother says. He doesn't like hookers. Sometimes my brother lists what he likes and what he doesn't like. Under "I like," Tiger, the cat, takes first place, I follow next. Under "I don't like," Principal V. and Doctor S. lead unbeaten, for superstitious reasons he never utters their horrible names and I'm not allowed to either; next come shepherds, hookers and bus drivers. Policemen are under "I like."

At the bus station stands a homeless man with crutches, a broken shoe in his hand. In front of him a policeman, who shouts at him to show his ID. Aunt Ella has given us twenty eggs. When we get home I make scrambled eggs for my brother and me. After a week my brother doesn't want to eat scrambled eggs anymore. We don't dare to get the sausages that hang in the pantry. We are afraid that later we won't be able to explain to our father and our mother where they have gone when they ask.

My brother is sucking at a white stone that looks like a bean. He's good at it, he doesn't swallow the stone. He tells the girls that his American uncle has given him a peppermint that doesn't melt. They believe him, look at him admiringly. I'm also going to look for a stone like that, which looks so pretty on my brother's pink tongue, between his teeth, white as chalk. But I can't find one.

We're eating lard. My skin is bursting. I don't know whether it's from the lard or the egg white I spread on my face since we have stopped eating the eggs. I spread the egg-yolk on the back of my hands and lips. Pieces of dry, crumbled egg yolk lie everywhere in the house and the yard. I'm cooking cocoa dumplings, polenta and instant goulash soup with dried vegetable squares in it. We eat it very hot. I have a blister on my tongue, my brother says later. At least he doesn't want to eat anymore that day.

Do you know that you're ugly, my brother says. Don't bother going there. They only take pretty ones.

Aunt Magdala gives me as a present a Pepita dress that reaches below the knee and highlights my thick calves. At the collar, at the seam, and at the sleeves it has black frills.

When I was a child, Aunt Magdala often stood me on the chest of drawers at her place and I had to recite "You Are like a Flower." She cried each time. I don't tell her that "You Are like a Flower" is not on my audition list. She is the only one who is not surprised that I want to become an actress. She seems to have a strong belief that it's possible. In the hospital my mother said to me she would pray that they send me back again.

Aunt Magdala tells me that she has seen our father in the village. He has been in the inn since yesterday playing cards. I am reflected in the window-pane and cut my hair straight with the trimmer. The trimmer was the only present my grandfather brought back from his trip to West Germany. I am wearing my father's earthen-brown wedding suit to the audition, even though it's a bit too short for me.

In town the asphalt reaches to the skin of the trees. I am walking around the roots in blue shoes.

The room we are waiting in isn't lit. The walls are panelled with dark wood and there's a chimney. The chimney is made of pale pink marble. Like in the castle. I put my hand on its shoulder. It fits perfectly. We are standing. The others around us are practicing movements. The floorboards are creaking gloomily under their bodies.

The other girls stare at my head. It is covered by an almost invisible golden fuzz. My ears. The only speck of light in the room shines on them. The boys don't look at me. They turn away. They are ashamed for me.

During the audition I pay attention to the *A*, I pronounce it as openly as I can. Finally, one of the men says: You have a dialect. Yes, I say. Why do I want to become an actress? I say, I come from a farm. The men don't pull faces. Then another man looks at my list and asks: The periodic table? I nod. I breathe air into my Sarastro lungs and sing: Ha- He-Li-Be-Be-Ce-NeO-Fe-Ne-Na-MgAl-Si-Pe-Se-ClAr . . .

Just say it. Word for word. Without heroics. Don't sob. Don't melt. Just say it. Word for word.

When you come from town and look at it from the bus, my village seems to consist of one single, entwined matter. From fibre, so brown and inextricable, like the wool in our clothes. When I stop at the edge of the fields in Father's suit and gaze back to the road, where only minutes ago the bus has discharged me into the brown dusk, the bus as well as the road have disappeared. And suddenly I realise that my brother is right: It is actually possible that there are times when we become invisible.

My fair head rolls like a low moon through the middle of the landscape. I wander across invisible fields. I think that I'm going to be an actress. I think, if I'm going to be an actress I have to pay attention to the *A* and not becoming invisible. I think of a stage as an undulating window-pane, a chest of drawers. I think of cocoa dumplings and lard. Of my brother and me. My hair as fertiliser on the field.

The field guard Kelemen is playing the accordion in the pub. My father has lost three pension payments already. Apart from me, there are only men here, and they were already drunk when I entered in my Pepita dress. Florian is here, and although he is afraid of my father, he requests a new polka and we dance on the little empty square in front of the entrance. My father doesn't take his eyes off the cards.

My brother is sitting on the bench next to Kelemen. His slanted eyes are red from the fruit schnapps and his face is white as chalk, as spider webs, his hair is yellow. I'm dancing polka with Florian. Take care, my brother says, he is a gypsy. So what, I say, and the boat planks stir up dust and bounce beneath our feet. You're going to be nothing but a hooker, my brother says in a deep voice. So what, I say and spin around with Florian, leg in leg. Polka after all is my favourite dance.

Ha-He-Li-Be!

FROM *In jeder Sprache sitzen andere Augen*
FROM *There Are Different Eyes Inside Each Language*

In the language of the village—so it appeared to me as a child—the words spoken by the people around me sat directly on the things they signified. Things were called exactly what they were, and they were exactly what they were called. An agreement reached for all time. For most people there were no gaps between word and object one had to look through and stare into nothingness, as if slipping out of one's skin into a void. Daily tasks were instinctive, wordlessly practised labour, the head did not follow the movements of the hand and didn't have its own deviating paths either. The head was there to carry the eyes and ears that were needed for work. The saying, "He's got his head on his shoulders so it won't rain down his throat," could be applied to everyone's daily life. Or could it? Why did my grandmother advise my mother, when there was nothing to do outside in winter and my father was reeling drunk for days on end, "If you think you can't take it anymore, tidy up the wardrobe." Silencing the head by moving clothes back and forth. Mother was supposed to fold and stack or hang her blouses and his shirts, her stockings and his socks, her skirts and his trousers side by side. Neatly together, their clothes were supposed to prevent his drinking himself out of this marriage.

Words accompanied work only if several people worked together, and each depended on the hands of the others. And not necessarily even then. Hard labour like carrying sacks, digging, hoeing, mowing with a scythe, was a school in silence. The body was too busy to exert itself with talk. Twenty, thirty people could be silent for hours. Sometimes I thought, watching them, now I'm watching what happens when people unlearn how to speak. They'll have forgotten all words by the time they're done with their labour.

What someone does need not be duplicated in words. Words hold up the movement of the hands, they stand squarely in the body's way—I knew that. But the incongruity between the outside at the hands and inside the head, the knowledge: now you're thinking something you're not entitled to and no one believes you're capable of; that was something else. It only ever came with fear. I wasn't more fearful than others but had, as they too, probably, all the groundless reasons to be afraid—head-built, thought-up reasons. But a thought-up fear isn't just imagined, it is valid if one has to grapple with it, as real as fear caused by the outside. One could also, since it's built entirely in the head, call it headless fear. Headless because it knows no explicit cause and has no remedy. Emil M. Cioran said that moments of groundless fear come closest to existence. The sudden search for meaning, the nervous fever, the shudder of the mind at the question: What is my life worth? Imperiously, this question tore into the usual, blinked in rather "ordinary" moments. I neither had to suffer hunger nor go barefoot; at night I lay in bed and fell asleep on clean, crisply ironed sheets. The prayer: "*Bevor ich mich zu Ruh begeb, / zu dir, oh Gott, mein Herz ich heb*"[1] was sung to me before the light was switched off. But then the tiled stove next to the bed became a water tower, the one with the wild wine, at the edge of the village. The beautiful poem by Helga M. Novak, "*Der Wilde Wein um den Wasserturm verfärbt sich ganz, wenn er verblüht ist wie die Unterlippe der Soldaten*,"[2] I didn't know back then. The prayer, which was supposed to calm me and draw me directly into sleep, had the opposite effect; it stirred up the head. I've therefore never understood, not later and to this day, how faith can calm people's fear, how it gives balance to some and helps to keep still the thoughts in the skull. Because each ever-so-often rattled-off prayer became a paradigm. It demanded the interpretation of my own state of mind. The feet's place is on the ground; slightly higher up are the stomach, the ribs, the head. On top, the hair. And how does one lift the heart to God through one's hair and a heavy ceiling? Why does Grandmother sing these words to me if she herself can't do what they demand?

The wild wine is called "Ink-grapes" in the dialect, because their black berries discolour the hands with stains that eat into the skin for days. The water tower next to the bed, its ink-grapes black, as deep sleep should be. I knew falling asleep meant to be drowned in ink. But I also knew that those who can't sleep have a bad conscience, have an uneasy load lying in their skulls. So that's what I had, but didn't

1. lit. "Before I go to bed, to you, my Lord, I lift my heart."

2. lit. "All the wild wine around the water tower discolours when it withers like the bottom lip of soldiers."

know why. Even in the village night outside there was ink. The tower had the land in its grip, it drew back the ground and the sky, and for all the people in the village in the ink there was only the one tiny, solid place, where they happened to find themselves just then. Frogs croaked from all directions, crickets frolicked, showed the way underground. And locked, so that no one escaped, the village into the echo of a box. I, like all children, was taken to see the dead. They were laid out in the best room of the house. They were visited one last time before they were taken to the cemetery. The coffins were open, the feet with the upright shoe soles pointed toward the door. Entering the door one walked once around the coffin, starting from the feet, and looked at the body. The frogs and crickets were at their service. At night they told the living something transparent that was meant to confuse their heads. I held my breath as long as I could to try and understand what they were saying. But then, in panic, I gasped for air. I wanted to understand, but not lose my head without getting it back again. Those who understand the transparent are grabbed by the feet, are gone from earth, I thought. The feeling of being prey in the village box to the feasting of the land also overwhelmed me on the days of glaring heat in the river valley where I had to tend cows. I had no watch, my clock was the train line to the city. Four trains passed through the valley each day, I wasn't allowed to return home until after the fourth. By then it was eight in the evening. By then even the sky began to chew grass and pull the valley up into it. I hurried to get away before it began. On those long days in a very large, brashly green valley, I asked countless times what my life was worth. I pinched red marks into my skin to find out what kind of material these legs and arms were made of, when God wanted his material back from me. I ate leaves and blossoms so that they became related to my tongue. I wanted us to be alike because they knew how to live and I did not. I addressed them by their names. The name "milk thistle" was meant to be a prickly plant with milk in its stalks. But the plant didn't appreciate the name, it didn't respond to it. I tried out invented names, "spike rib," "needle throat," in which neither "milk" nor "thistle" appeared. The deception of all the false names for the right plant opened

up the gap into emptiness. The humiliation of talking aloud with myself, not with the plant. On the four passing trains the windows were
pulled down, short-sleeved passengers stood inside, I waved. I went
as close to the train line as I could to see some of the travellers' faces.
Groomed townspeople were on the train, some ladies sparkled with
jewellery and red nail polish. Once the train had passed, my flutter-
ing dress stuck to my body again, my head felt hazy from the suddenly interrupted airflow, as if after the crash landing of a flying carousel,
the eyes hurt in my head. The eyeballs, as though they'd been pulled
a bit too far from the forehead; chilled by the slipstream, they'd become too big for the eye sockets. My breath was faint, the skin on my
arms and legs dirty, scratched, the fingernails green and brown. After each train I felt abandoned, disgusted and had an even closer look
at myself. Then the valley sky became a large blue, and the pasture
a large green piece of dirt, and I a little piece of dirt in between that
didn't count. The word "lonely" doesn't exist in the dialect, only the
word "alone." And it was called *alleenig* and it sounds like *wenig*[1]—
and that's how it was.

That's also how it was in the middle of the cornfield. Knobs
with old-people-hair one could braid plaits with, and broken yellow
teeth—the kernels of corn. One's body rustled, was as paltry as the
empty wind in the dust. The throat inside dry from thirst, overhead
a foreign sun like a tray in a distinguished household upon which a
guest is served a glass of water. Even now I'm saddened by long cornfields, I close my eyes whenever I drive past cornfields in a train or by
car, gripped by the sudden fear that upright corn fields spread around
the whole world.

I hated the stubborn field that feasted on wild plants and animals
in order to feed domesticated plants and animals. Each field was a bor-
derless, spread-out panopticon of ways to die, a blossoming funeral
feast. Each landscape practised death. Flowers mimicked the necks,
noses, eyes, lips, tongues, fingers, belly-buttons, nipples of people,
didn't rest, borrowed body parts, waxen-yellow, chalk-white, blood-
red, bruise-blue, squandered, paired with green, whatever wasn't
theirs. These colours threaded through the skin of the dead as they

1. lit. "sparse," little, few. withers like the bottom lip of soldiers."

pleased. The living were so stupid and craved them and on the corpses they blossomed because the flesh surrendered. From visiting the dead I was familiar with blue fingernails, the yellow gristle in greenish earlobes that plants had already stuck their teeth into, impatiently embarking on the work of decomposition in the midst of the best room in the house, not waiting for the grave. On the roads of this village, between houses, wells and trees, I thought: These are the tassels of the world, one ought to live on the carpet, it's made of asphalt, and only in the city. I didn't want to be caught out by the blooming panopticon that squandered all colours; didn't want to put my body at the disposal of this voracious summer blaze camouflaged by blossoms. What I wanted was to move away from the tassels and onto the carpet where the asphalt underfoot was so tight that death from below wasn't creeping around ankles. I wanted to ride on trains like a lady from the city with bright red polished nails, walk on asphalt with dainty shoes like lizard heads, listen to the dry clip-clop of footsteps as I'd noticed on two visits to the doctor in town. I couldn't accept being alive amid the feasting orbit of the plants, the reflection of leaf-green on my skin, although peasants were all I knew. I always saw that the field only fed me because it wanted to devour me later. It remained a mystery to me how one's life could be entrusted to a place that showed at each and every turn that one was a candidate in the panopticon of dying.

It was a failure that I wasn't convinced of what I did, and that no one thought me capable of what was going through my head. I had to tear open the moment to such an extent that nothing humanly possible could fill it. I provoked the naked advance of transiency, was unable to find the right balance, to stick to the ordinary.

It is compromising to slip out of one's skin into emptiness. I wanted to come close to my surroundings but wore myself out, let it tear me up so much that I couldn't put myself together again. Incestuous, as it appears to me today. I was yearning for "normal contact" and blocked it off because I couldn't let things rest. I had an urgent need to keep still inside but didn't understand how to bring it about. I think it didn't show on the outside. It never came to my mind to talk about it. The deviations in my head had to be kept hidden. Besides, there were no words for it in the dialect apart from these two adjectives: "lazy" for the physical side of things and "profound" for the psychological side. As for myself, I had no words for it either. I still don't have any. It's not true that there are words for everything. And that one always thinks in words isn't true either. To this day, there's much that I haven't thought in words, I haven't found any, not in village German, not in town German, not in Romanian, not in East or West German. And not in books. The inner districts don't coincide with language, they drag people to places where words can't reside. Often it's what matters most about which nothing can be said anymore, and the impulse to talk about it only works well because it is missing the point. The belief that talking can help sort out confusion, I've only come across in the West. Talking neither sorts out life in the cornfield nor life on the asphalt. And the belief that what doesn't make sense can't be endured I've also only ever come across in the West.

What can talking do? If the greater part of life isn't right anymore, even words collapse. I've seen my own words collapse. And I was certain that the words I didn't have would collapse right along with them if I'd had them. The nonexistent ones would have become like the existing ones that already collapsed. I never knew how many words one needed to completely cover the forehead's deviation. A deviation that immediately distanced itself from the words found for it. Which words are they, and how quickly would they have to be at the ready and take turns with others to catch up with one's thoughts. And what would catching up mean? Thinking after all speaks altogether differently with itself than words speak with it.

Still the wish "to be able to say it." If I hadn't always had that wish it would never have come to my trying out names for the milk thistle in order to address it by its proper name. Without that wish I wouldn't have caused the estrangement around me as a result of closeness gone wrong.

Objects have always been important to me. Their appearance belonged to the image of the people who owned them, just as the people themselves. They always and inseparably belong to how and what a person was. They are the outermost part of a person, lifted off their skin. And if they outlive their owners, the absent person moves into the remaining objects. After my father died the hospital handed over his dentures and his glasses. At home his tiniest screwdrivers were in a kitchen drawer with the cutlery. As long as he was alive my mother told him every other day that tools didn't belong there, that he ought to put them somewhere else. After he died they stayed there for years. Now my mother didn't mind the sight of the screwdrivers. If their owner wasn't sitting at the table anymore, at least his tools ought to be among the cutlery. A timidity came over her hands, generous exceptions undermined her sense of order. Now, I thought, he would be allowed to eat with his screwdrivers instead of knife and fork, if he were to return to this table. And even the stubborn apricot trees in the courtyard weren't ashamed to bloom. In a strange way, emotions are often apportioned to the outside. To a few objects that, for no reason, are suitable to illustrate the remembering inside one's head. It involves taking detours. Neither dentures nor glasses represented the absence of Father, but the screwdrivers and the apricot trees. I penetrated the trees so irrationally with my eyes that the still barren, short branches became the spitting images of the small screwdrivers if I stared long enough into the trees. I was grown-up then, and still everything got tangled just as deviously as in the past.

Emine Sevgi Özdamar

MUTTERZUNGE
MOTHER TONGUE

In my language, tongue is called: language.

Tongue has no bones, wherever it is twisted it will twist.
I sat with my twisted tongue in this city, Berlin. Negro café, Arab
customers, the stools are too high, legs dangle. An old croissant sits
wearily on a plate, I give baksheesh right away, the waiter mustn't be
ashamed. If only I knew when I lost my mother tongue. My mother
and I once spoke in our mother tongue. My mother said to me, "You
see, you speak like, you think that you are telling everything, but suddenly you skip unsaid words, then you speak calmly again; I skip along
with you, then I breathe calmly." Then she said, "You left half of your
hair in *Alamania*."
Now I only remember mother sentences she said in her mother tongue
if I imagine her voice, the sentences themselves come to my ears like
a foreign language I've learned well. I also asked her why Istanbul had
become so dark, she said, "Istanbul always had these lights, your eyes
are used to *Alamania* lights." I still remember a Turkish mother and
the words she said in our mother tongue. She was the mother of a
boy in prison not sleeping at night because he waited to be taken to
his hanging. This mother said, "I came from the hospital eleven years
ago. I saw: the garden was full of policemen, my head jumped, I asked
neighbours. They're probably here for your son, they said. I went to
the garden, to the first policeman. Why have you come into my garden, I said. Your son has been caught, he said. Why should my son
have been caught, do you actually have search warrant papers, I said, I
am illiterate. He said yes. Go inside the house then, search, I said. The
house filled up with them, I sat on my haunches, stayed there; when I
asked, what happened to my son, they said, your son is an anarchist."
This mother didn't know how many times in eleven years she had
cried, twice she fell on her knees, once when she saw her son in prison
for the first time and couldn't recognize him. The second time when
he had to hear the word "hanging," standing up.

"I never went to court, last court, the judges will speak, they said. His father went there, came back; as he walked through the door I saw it in his face, all the neighbours followed behind him, we cried together, our *Hodscha* from alley mosque stood like half a man on his knees, cried; the ash tray, as thick as two fingers, broke from the middle in two that day, I heard a 'shasht', the ash-tray lay right in front of me." Even these sentences, from the mother of a hanged man, I remember only as if she had said the words in German.

The writings also came to my eyes like a foreign script I'd learned well. A newspaper extract. "Workers shed their own blood." Strikes were banned, workers cut their fingers, laid their shirts underneath the dripping blood, they wrapped their dry bread in the bloodied shirts, sent it to the Turkish military, this I also remember as if the news were written in several newspapers at a kiosk; you saw it in passing, took a photograph, dropped it.

If only I knew at what moment I lost my mother tongue. Once I walked around that prison in Stuttgart, there was a lawn, a single bird flew past the cell windows, a prisoner in a blue track suit clung to the bars, he had a very soft voice, he spoke in the same mother tongue, said to someone loudly, "Brother Yashar, did you see it?" The other, who I couldn't see, said "Yes, I saw."
To see: *Görmek*.
I stood on the lawn and smiled. We were so far away from each other. They saw me like a big needle in nature, I didn't know what they meant by seeing, was it me or a bird? From a prison one can only see, grab, feel, catch. Picking, that's not possible.
Görmek: To see.

I remember another word in my mother tongue, it was in a dream. I was in Istanbul in a wooden house, there I met a friend, a communist, he doesn't laugh, I tell him about someone who tells stories from the corner of his mouth, shallow. Communist-friend said, "Everyone speaks like that." I said, "What do you have to do to speak with

depth?" He said, "*Kaza gecirmek*, experience life-accidents."
Görmek and *Kaya gecirmek*.

Another word in my mother tongue once came in a dream. A train
travels, stops, there are arrests outside, dogs are barking, three conduc-
tors are coming, I think about whether I should say: "I am Italian." I
want to hide my ID, which states *ISCI* (worker) as my profession, I
think, if I can identify myself as student or artist I'll pass the search;
there is a photocopier, large as a room, it prints out a very large self
portrait of me as an *ISCI*.
Görmek. Kaya gecirmek, ISCI.

I sat at a table once in an Inter-City train restaurant, a man sat at another avidly reading a book, I thought, what is he reading? It was the
menu. Perhaps I lost my mother tongue in the IC restaurant.
In the beginning I couldn't look at the Kölner cathedral here. When
the train arrived in Köln, I always closed eyes, but one time I opened
an eye; at just the moment I saw it, the cathedral looked at me, then a
razor blade entered my body, moved inside, then the pain was gone, I
opened my second eye also. Perhaps it was there that I lost my mother tongue.
Get up, go to the other Berlin, Brecht was the first person why I came
here; perhaps there I can remember when I lost my mother tongue.
In the corridor between two Berlins, a photo booth.
I am at the Berliner Ensemble, canteen.
My boots are crunching like a cowboy's in a trailer. The canteen workers are smoking, talking about pots and plates, beer barrels wait outside, gas bottles; everyone is talking about work.

Get up. Walk on fingertips to Turkey, sit on a divan, Grandmother
next to me. Sit in the Turkish bath in Istanbul. The Gypsy bath wom-
en are going to wash me. It was a hooker bath, once a Gypsy woman
washed me, she asked, "Which house are you working in, beautiful?"
I worked in the communist commune, one day the police came, I was
the only girl, the inspector asked me, "These blokes here, are they all

walking over you?" I said, "Yes, they are all walking over me, but are walking carefully."

Inspector said, "Don't you have a heart for your father, I also have a daughter your age, may Allah curse you all, inshallah."

They also brought Mahir's brother into the police corridor; Mahir, who had been made famous in the papers as a bandit. By that time they had killed Mahir with bullets. Mahir's brother was sitting there as if he had something bitter in his mouth and he couldn't spit it out; he wore a very thin shirt, I had a dark jumper with a turtle-neck.

"Brother, put it on." Mahir's brother looked at me as if I was speaking a foreign language. Why am I standing in half of Berlin? Going to look for this boy? It's been seventeen years, the milk they drank from their mothers was taken out of their noses.

I'm going to return to the other Berlin. I'm going to learn Arabic, it used to be our script; after the war of liberation, 1927, Atatürk banned Arabic script and Latin letters appeared; my grandfather only knew Arabic script, I only knew the Latin alphabet, that is, if my grandfather and I were mute and could only talk in writing, we couldn't tell each other stories. First back to Grandfather perhaps, then I may find the way to my mother and mother tongue.

Inshallah.

There was a great master of the Arabic script in West Berlin.

Ibni Abdullah.

Ilma Rakusa /169

Die Tür zum Meer
The Door to the Sea

And I imagined that it was easy to describe. The sea below me. Blue, no, white, no, green, no, at one with the sky, no, frizzy, no, smooth, no, all of this and more. How do I capture its motion. It is so beautiful. I'll leave it blank.

The first time, I took the way along the Baroque steps steep, but swift. I crossed the Jesuit square, children rode bikes there between the gravel and the grass, even the trees unsightly. I headed for the edge. I reached the circular wall and stood in its shade. I walked along the wall, across an improvised football field, the children make do with only a few meters, just let me pass through thanks. The way narrows, one step, a second one, and where might this pine get its water from, growing amid the stone. The black, iron-barred door. It is open. This must be it. I step through the opening in the wall and see it all around, in terrific brightness, flooding and free, within grasp—jump! The sea. I sat down on the small plateau and watched. Nothing else but that. I closed my eyes, it was here, far down, crashing against the cliffs.

Then, with the heat, the women came, one after the other, in black or patterned aprons, in slippers; crawled out of the shady houses and sat down in the sun. Their voices drowned out the surf. A buzzing carpet above the shimmering sea. They were used to the sight. They had to talk about deaths, knitting patterns, that also. They worked themselves into a high pitch. I searched for the Montenegrin mountains in the haze. Not to be made out. I left.

The second time I took Neda along. Not up the steep steps this time but along "underworld street." She laughs, as if this street was just right for her. Above the sea she doesn't laugh anymore. She looks at it with a steady gaze. And? The blue. And? I can't bear its beauty. Yes, I say. There was something, she says, that you don't know about. We are looking at the sea. I had a son, she says, he is dead.

I stroke her red hair, the white, protruding ears, helpless. Twofold clinical death, she says, the heart. Whose heart? Mine, she says. The child was born, it died four weeks after birth. Neda, I say.

The sea lies underneath us like a plastic sheet, an element preoccupied with itself.

No, she says. Never again. The doctors forbade it.

For your sake.

What am I to me? They don't guarantee for the child. And that—

Yes.

For three months she hadn't been able to talk about it with anyone. For three months she had been sitting in her flat petrified, crying, life split into two, into before and after; she had not been able to bring the ends together again. The one Neda comforts the other, encourages her. No one knew anything about it.

What is painful about beauty? I ask.

She still looks at the sea.

The memory, she says. In that darkest of tunnels, colours lit up, indescribable. Death.

We heard no sea, no gossiping women, the sun stood in the west, copper red, Neda's pigtail burned, I pushed her to the balustrade, no, she screamed, not face to face! and darted backward through the door. Look there, the blue mountains, I said conciliatorily. But she headed for the underworld, the underworld street, do you understand now?

The third time I went on my own to escape the press of tourists. I slipped through the opening in the wall, the wind rushed at my face. Cantankerous, the sea. Never before had I thought abyss; now I did. And my thoughts wandered back to the Jesuit church, which had been given a nuptial decoration for the resurrected one, with sweet carnations. The railing was almost useless. Swung fairly into the sky, but to the left and right everything was possible, everything. I closed my eyes. I waited for the voices of the women. I longed for them to be here. Someone came. I looked up. An adolescent came and lay down on the stone with the inscription "free." I didn't ask if he was cold. I opened the book and read:

He must have fallen asleep. The shadows of the hedge covered the entire square of the prospective terrace. M. lay in its shelter, without memory of his gradual progress. He must have fallen asleep, again and again. The shadow of the hedge thicker than a wall . . . He had approached the abyss in vain. He would never, never do it again.

He was sleeping. The other, over there, the liberated, the sea-ish one, the adolescent, he was sleeping. Why was I reading? I wasn't ashamed that he had stolen my view, was I? Neda's courage had left me in the face of the monstrous, the sea.

Then the first came, the second came, the old woman came: Ah, miss, back again! But why in black, perhaps in mourning? No, I say, thanks, no. And the second: Fashion, don't you know that. And the old one: Are you from far away? Rather, I say. Then, she says, have a good trip, and laughs.

It wasn't the last time. I met the sea at the harbour, in the fishermen's bay, but only here, behind the gate, deep underneath the walls, it was the sea. Mine. Neda had gone away. Mira wasn't afraid of anything. She said: Show me the sea. I led her across the football field unhindered, I pushed her softly through the door. She was radiant and silent. She sat down where Neda had sat, with her back to the sun, looked at the sea. Gentle, she said, I know the Pacific. I asked myself who she was. Can't she give voice to her fear? And could I? I pointed to her belt: You won't get far with a plastic knife. She laughs. Or do you? The belts, I say, make you feel safe. You tie yourself up, the wider the belt the better. Certainly, she says. I didn't say Amazon. I only thought that this dainty body denies its daintiness. Compulsion? I asked quietly. This is how I want it, she said, I am practicing resistance. While she remained enigmatic the sun wandered westward. The women were already sitting on the stone and knitted. Mira took no notice of them, she asked, Are you lonely? Her eyes shone mischievously, I didn't understand. Doesn't matter, she said. Anyway, I said, how am I to know, out of the blue? You just are, she said. I gave in.

We stopped talking. I watched her profile, she watched the sea. In the meantime, the afternoon was passing. The swallows began to circle. I asked myself who she was. And in desperation, or from love, I opened the book.

I bought a house, I read. *The place is beautiful. You imagine being in Greece. The trees around the house are mine. One of them, gigantic, provides so much shade that I will never suffer from the heat again. I want to have a terrace built. From this terrace you can see the lights of D. at night . . .*

There are moments here of a perfect, diverse, yet precise light, which settles on a single object, passionately . . .

The sea, she said.

You, she said.

I took her hand, and we left the plateau. It was the last time.

DURCH SCHNEE
THROUGH SNOW

In December, during a fierce snowstorm, Anna Sergeyevna decided to put an end to the lie. She would stay in Moscow. She would write a long letter to her husband and confess her love for Gurov. There was nothing disgraceful about it, only her despondence was disgraceful. She was hurrying now. Clarity, she mumbled. Whatever is going to happen. She flailed about exitedly with her arms. Clarity. And her small body twitched.

In the evening she sat in her room in the boarding house and wrote. Outside the storm was raging, but she didn't hear the wind, heard nothing.

"... You hardly know me. You married a pale girl, offered her space, and the fences took care of the rest. I was never to blossom into a woman. You the provider, I your pupil. The years in S went by. A shadow carousel. I wasn't unhappy, I didn't know what happiness was.

Have you ever tousled my hair? Dreamed to the end my abandoned dreams? You, a lover of dashing operettas, assigned a little place for me. There I sat with the spitz. How was I to embark for new shores when the river was frozen?

And then the sea. The white sun. The trees, in which birds were kissing. I was on my own and so free. I felt to be in a sparkling white story. Walked up and down the hills between dog roses, and often along the quays. Bay leaves, the ships out at sea, as if I was at another end of the world. Until late at night. And wanted to get ever closer to this life. Into this moving, burning region.

But do you believe me? Believe me that I sang furtively. And waved at a cloud. Short swaying step, eyes straight ahead. Little by little nothing was as it used to be anymore.

This is how Gurov met me. He recognized me without a word. My appearance aroused his pity, but my inner hunger tempted him. And I? I despised myself for having deceived you. But I knew there was no turning back. Dissolute or not, guilty or not, I held on to a morsel of happiness. Didn't want to throttle the brand-new adventure, the Sundays and fleeting nights. Grieved and lusted. He endured my doubts. This was the beginning of our love.

You think I acted recklessly? No and no again. I compromised what held together no more, and it reeked, for it was mouldering underneath. Yet I returned home to you. To a homely state. It was base. My heart flown off, head in the clouds, lips pursed inward. And you didn't ask. You thought, it always comes good in the end. Or were you making counterplans?

I was banished from each and every heaven. Whenever the air stood still I hoped for a quiet way out. It didn't come. I pretended to be going to a gynaecologist in Moscow. I deceived both of us. You were generous. Or are you a lackey? I don't know who you are. For years there has been this dread between us, and outside the night. Little remains therefore: a few memories, the residue of a lost phrase.

I'll stay in Moscow, but there is no heaven here either. The girl of the past asks your forgiveness. She has learned: sadness, and that rivers flow underground. Now the time for daylight has come.

Please find rest at a southern sea.

Spitz is my comfort. He doesn't know a thing. Only his eyes are getting ever smaller. Yes."

Anna Sergeyevna closed and stared in front of herself. As if into an unfathomable darkness, as if into her own chamber of the heart. I'm dying, she thought for a moment. The keys are gone. But then she thought of Gurov, who knew nothing and to whom she would reveal tomorrow that she'd stay. She wasn't empty air. Here she was, even if in his way.

What will happen will happen, she mumbled. Somewhere in the closet hung her few dresses, lay a keepsake of her childhood. I have no home. This is how it begins.

Gurov was surprised that she didn't open. Had she been taken ill or gone out? He felt responsible for her because with her gentleness she had confused these times and planted paradise in his brain. That's how children, how sorry fools walk the world. Unforgiving. He belonged to her. Why?

Snow. It falls on everything, the footpath, the questions, ones own despondence. White or grey, large flakes and wet. Gurov ran. If only he could float, escape all gravity.

Christ! Spitz!

He shouted.

You here?

She stood at a distance and smiled.

Moved and alarmed he looked at her. The small woman, the big child, his health and affliction, his ark and despair.

Come, let's have some tea, she said cheerfully. He didn't believe a word she said.

Breathlessly they arrived at the boarding house. She moved lightly, greeted the porter fleetingly but self-assured. In the room she threw off her overcoat before Gurov could as much as touch her shoulder.

Tea then.

Isn't there something more important?

She hadn't kissed him. He began pacing the room. Remained silent. When the tea steamed from the glasses she pulled him onto a chair.

I'm staying, she said, almost toneless. For good.

He was startled. You?

His pupils dilated. She looked into his frozen, frightened face and for a moment she felt pity for him.

Inconvenient?

As if shaking off a dream his upper body jerked, he got up and walked to the door.

But how could you—

Yes, she said.

Had she expected that he would throw his arms around her?

There she sat, and he stood. And between them was time, not to be regained. Or perhaps, if he'd overcome his cowardice, if he also put an end to the lie—

She smiled to herself. How strange it all was, how awry. She smiled and didn't notice that he cried.

SOMMER
SUMMER

Suddenly there are facial expressions in the sand, and it's bright. Overly bright behind the curtain. A hot sky hangs above the city. The walnut tree in the courtyard of the *Kunstwerke* is being watered, even the pavement, for cooling; each shadow is occupied. Children are digging or carrying bells in their hands. The swallows are screeching. Iced cucumber soup is the order of the day. Underneath the awnings the young are dozing, and modern floristry, that also. Do hydrangeas have a heart? Let's wait for now, with questions, with everything, until well into the evening, when the open-air cinema is setting up its wide-angle screen directly in front of the Alte Museum, in front of the Schinkel gables. Deckchair unfolded, Ikea brand, ultramarine. With a white circle. Or striped. A Mediterranean expedition between the colonnades. And the first breeze picks up. And the blinking face of Björk, large, bespectacled. She says she's seen enough, she doesn't need to see any more of this world. Just like that, thrown into the crowd. We are not indifferent, we look as if entranced. At the dancer, going blind, at the destitute murderess, at the rope. The night sky already blue, the chirping subsides. Overarching, the German backdrop. *Mit hinten Linden*, laterally damaged building. The outlook is rumbling inside. Underneath the neon stars, the film revs up three times, in vain. It manoeuvres itself into the pool of death. And we are pretty cooled down. Then vacating, vacating, on the way back home ambivalence and a lone cricket. Pretty cooled down. The blood chirps only at dawn, restlessly. And prepares itself for a record heat wave. The runners in the streets look incidental. In shorts. Calm, though, the Jews from Adass Jisroel: black trousers, white shirt, dark blue skirt, white blouse, headscarf, the girl with a staggering gait. And all of them certain. The way they cross the Tucholsky as a clan. I look at them. Saturday, Shabbat. Enlivened by their readings. I myself am faint. From doubt and ozone, from. I take the number two, travel into no-man's-land, through the light swaths, avenues. Where the apartment blocks are glistening, eastish. Where the lawn is rusting and the socialist friezes are haggard. Ulan Bator. Minsk. Superbly dismal, this steppe. Only the light is splendid, fairy blue somehow. Transparent above the roofs. In the Friedrichshain Volkspark the ravers cower. Next to the pond, in the shadow of the North Korean bell. The legacies of the GDR stand on hills here, in depressions. Faithfully. In front of the restaurant pavilion a dismal afternoon band. Otherwise the district is greening, a green city lung is what we need. To escape the dust heat. We need zoos and moors and. Winding paths up and down. And lots of flora and a friend underneath a linden tree. Fair hope, but. Linden, poplar, plane trees, all here, children, prams, mothers, bird sound. Only make-me-happy is missing. That's how I walk through the district, Bötzow, half-restored, slightly staggering, always following the shadow, into the evening. Which doesn't want to be an evening. Heartburn in front of small pubs, from which American English chirps here and there. The shops closed, the pensioners sluggish in their cubbyholes. There is the melancholy of stagnation, no wind, the time of day undecided. Toward Berg the storeys of the houses rise, they are towering already. Wörtherstraße, Rykestraße. Water tower. Grand bourgeois. I mean with balconies, awnings, broken-up friezes, with. Evergreen. Couples on the move, in the Pasternak, the scene, lolling about, recapitulating. Farther on. What's the option. Ambling, the head engages in details. "Borschtsch" is written on the slate, a frantic white spitz has a screw loose and someone is bawling. This then would be a constellation. Here and now, corner of Kollwitzplatz. My lover has sharp little teeth, if he is my lover at all. Flashes through my ambling mind. Haven't seen him for ages. And. Company. A motorbike roars past, the pushbikes are singing. Sand in the joints, sand. Not even Triest had this to offer, the childhood city. Further, alder and aspen trees, brick stone red. Which pile up at times to churches, agnostic. Or create loft floors. The city is carnivore. The city bursts its sentences. Flows into grass edges, fallows, spills. Then we are somewhere. Between Swinemünder and Swinemünder, with a stripe of evening red. Stillness. Here the footpaths offer someone single so much freedom that he cries. He comes to and down with his baggage. Meanwhile the heat is abating. Directionless. Overhead, the yelling of swifts in fast formation. Hesitation. To the Zionskirche or return or. No one calls, want to say, waits. So everything from the beginning, repeated. Tendency downhill. To the former Scheunenviertel. Where the Eastern Jews passed on their misfortune, squashed together like herrings. And where instead of doss-houses, swanky new buildings now stand, dumped vacancies. Office and floor space en masse. The evening is fed up with it. The evening falls into the block. Veils the children's swing and a perished Trabi. Soon night will follow. I meander through the Mulackei; Filomena's bar, geared up, awakes. The latecomers are closing in, many single folk. With a heightened readiness to couple. During happy hour drinks or beer or. Cheers. Only the devil knows what's in store for me.

EINE LEERE FLASCHE
AN EMPTY BOTTLE

Our apartment in Tokyo, which was in a housing estate, carried the number two-six-two-zero-three. There were many girls of my age in the estate. One of the girls in particular caught my attention because she referred to herself as *boku*, a boy. We went to primary school together. Most girls at that age referred to themselves as *atashi*; a few precocious girls already as *watashi*; and a girl from a distinguished family used the word *atakushi*—this word smelled of cypress wood. Most of the boys called themselves *boku*, but a few cheeky or proud boys said *ore*. Of course there was no boy at this age who would have referred to himself as *watashi* or *watakushi*. It would have sounded ridiculous, they had to be much older for that.

I had difficulties with all of these words meaning "I." I felt neither like a girl nor a boy. As an adult, you can seek refuge in the gender-neutral word *watashi*, but until then, you are forced to be a boy or a girl. How simple my childhood would have been, if I had spoken another language—German, for instance. I could have simply said *ich* all the time. You don't have to feel either female or male to use the word *ich*. In my childhood I avoided words that can be used for *ich* in Japanese. If I wanted to emphasise that it was I who wanted something I used the words "this side": "As far as this side is concerned, it'd be nice if we went to the zoo tomorrow. As far as my sister is concerned, it won't be particularly convenient but doable. So we are going to the zoo tomorrow." I felt like a riverbank and on the opposite side of the river I saw my interlocutor. Between us was a river. The water was deep and turbulent, but if you wanted to it was possible to cross the river. The space between the German words *ich* and *du*, on the other hand, remains abstract; it is impossible to cross.

The girl who used the word *boku* mastered a few enviable tricks and was therefore respected by the other children. She could form a spoon shape with her tongue, jump from the balcony of the first floor, touch poisonous, colourful worms and spiders with her bare hands, blow the grass-blade flute and even play the piano. One day I asked the girl directly why she said *boku*. The girl simply answered: "Because most of the time I feel I am a *boku*. To be honest, there are moments now and again when I feel like a girl, but it's rare."

In weather reports they talk about so-called perceived temperatures: Depending on how strong the wind blows or how humid the air is, one and the same temperature can be perceived as higher or lower. Likewise, there is probably a perceived gender. On a windy day on the Pacific I felt more male than usual, on a sultry August day, however, I definitely was a girl.

"Don't you ever eat ice cream with fruit?" I asked the girl. "Of course," she answered and grinned. "Then you're a girl after all!" I replied. A big bowl of ice cream with colourful pieces of fruit was, in those days, considered a dish exclusively for girls and women. A boy or a man had to eat such things secretly and in shame.

The girl who called herself *boku* wore boys' shoes and had male cartoon characters on her pencils. Although her satchel was red, like the other girls', her umbrella was blue and had a picture of a robot on it, so it was male. "Do you have girl chopsticks or boy chopsticks at home?" I asked the girl. She shrugged her shoulders and revealed to me that she had chopsticks with Obakyu. The cartoon character Obakyu— just as with Pokémon today—was thought of as for boys and for girls. Unlike the girl who called herself *boku*, I could not identify as *boku*. Boys were alien to me, I only played with girls, but without feeling myself to be a girl.

Later, when I was studying, a friend told me that he always referred to himself as *boku* and could therefore fall in love with a man, who used the word *ore*, without having homosexual potential. The men who referred to themselves as *ore* seemed to have the characteristics he himself had not, and therefore fascinated him. He couldn't explain what these characteristics were. In this society a *boku* had a different place than an *ore*, he said, "that's why they behave differently." After he told me this, I came to realize that *ore* men had a different physical affect on me than *boku* men. There were at least four genders among adults, I said to him: *ore, boku, atashi* and *watashi*.

At some stage I lost track of the girl who called herself "*boku*." I also lost track of the problem of self-reference. Because I moved to Europe and found the word *ich*, which doesn't require these kinds of thoughts. An *ich* doesn't need to have a specific gender: no age, no status, no history, no disposition, no character. Everyone can simply call oneself *ich*. The word consists only of what I say or, to be more precise, of the fact that I say something at all. The word refers only to the speaker without adding any further information about him. *Ich* became my favourite word. I wanted to feel as light and empty as this word. I wanted to speak, that is, release vibrations in the air with my voice, without having to decide which gender I belong to.

I also like the fact that an *ich* begins with an *i*, a simple stroke, like the outset of a brushstroke, touching the paper and at the same time announcing the opening of a speech. *Bin*[1] is a nice word too. The word *bin* also exists in Japanese, it sounds exactly the same and means "a bottle." When I begin to tell a story with the two words *ich bin*, a space opens up, the *ich* is the touch of the brush, and the bottle is empty.

1. "Am"

MUSIK DER BUCHSTABEN
LETTER MUSIC

There is mail from France in my postbox. I open it and find a poem from Veronique Vassiliou inside. As I've never studied French, it's not surprising that I don't understand the text. Still, it seems strange to me that I understand absolutely nothing. After all, I know all the letters that appear in the text. I don't understand Chinese either, for instance, but when I see the character for "human," 人, I know at least that there is a human being. And how does a human being look in a French sentence?

I recognise the letter *d* at once and still understand nothing. It forms exactly half of a word, yet I can't understand even a quarter of its meaning. Is it possible that I get no information at all from a letter I know?

A language one hasn't learned is a transparent wall. It is possible to look through it into the distance because there is no meaning getting in the way. Each word is infinitely open, it can mean anything.

I see the word *du*. It is hard to believe that it has nothing to do with the German word *du*. A *du* one doesn't know can mean anything: a bag of grain, a Barbie doll, a pigeon or a door. No matter what I imagine it to be, the two letters *d* and *u* remain what they are. Perhaps the letters aren't interested at all in what they mean in a country. In Germany they mean this, in France that. They are travellers, over and again understood differently on their journey, depending on which language they spend the night in. But their bodies remain the same, namely a *d*, a semi-circle with a raised arm, and a *u*, an empty vessel. The word *blanc* follows the word *du*. It looks familiar. Wasn't the word written on a pencil I marvelled at in the window of a stationery shop? But what could the word mean? Brand names become familiar quickly; no one contemplates their meaning.

I skip a few words and find another one that also seems familiar to me: *bleu*. It appears in the menu of a fish restaurant. I think I know now. That is, I know nothing but I'm getting to the category of colours.

Fortunately, the foreignness of this language isn't too great. Although the words are different, the categories are identical. What would I do if there was a language in which the colour blue was understood as a tactile sense and white as a smell? In that case I probably couldn't do anything else but list the words and close my eyes. In the past the German expression *Ich weiß*[1] always made me think of the colour *weiß*.[2] *Ich weiß* meant: "I, paper-white." The *I* becomes white like a blank piece of paper, if this *I* knows something.

1. "I know"
2. "White"

I peruse the French text further. There are still more words that I notice: *horizontale, immobiles*. I think I understand these two words. In a short word external similarities don't count. But long words are rarely similar by accident. So, the longer the word, the more external its meaning.

A language one doesn't understand is read externally. Its appearance is taken seriously. The face of a French text looks rounder than a German one. The angular shoulders of the capital letters that lend each line an architectural character are missing.

Suddenly, from the round ripples of the small letters, the capital *B* emerges twice. Like two bass notes rising powerfully. Two words leap at my eyes. I understand them unquestionably: "Bach" and "Bartók." The music has reached me with the immediacy of proper nouns, it is untranslatable but present at this place at this moment.

I know that soon I'm going to receive a raw translation of this text. I am glad to have lived with only the indecipherable original for a few days, still I'm looking forward to the next mail delivering the meaning. Then the raw translation is going to produce energy like raw material. Perhaps I'll receive an interlinear translation, which will free me from the linearity of language. If I'll translate this text one day, I would want to encounter music. Although the music is present already, in Bach and Bartók, it has to be met once more in translation, through a long detour, with the help of dictionaries, conversations and dreams. By such a long detour of translation I would want to encounter the magic illegibility of a poem again.

Yoko Tawada

Der Apfel und die Nase
The Apple and the Nose

1. Wordplay, combining *Fantast* (fantasy, phantom) with *Tasten* (keys/keyboard).

How do you write in Japanese on the computer? You type the *Fantasten*,[1] you don't type the characters you want to write because there aren't any. There can't be any, they are too numerous for that. Instead there are alphabetical letters, and you type those. You pretend to be writing in the alphabet. But in actual fact you write a word as it is pronounced. Of course you can't write like you speak, just like you can't paint a soup the way it tastes. Therefore you have to write it so that the word would sound similar if an American would try to read it out loud. This process is called alphabetic transcription. Of course it is unlikely that an American turns up incidentally and tries to read the freshly typed word. Why should she do that? Therefore, so as not to have to rely on a rather improbable coincidence, the computer company has, with a forbidden fruit, lured a woman into the trap and locked her up in the casing of the computer. To this very day, an apple the woman has nibbled at back then is visible at the edge of the computer screen.

The computer tries to transcribe the words written in the alphabet into Japanese characters. But it finds it difficult. After all, there are about 8,000 characters sitting in the box. Many groups of words look identical in the alphabetical transcription, but they each have to be written differently as an ideogram. The computer can only choose the right symbol if it can understand the content of the text. It can actually do a lot, it can even understand and answer my question, if it isn't too poetical. Sometimes it gives me the feeling that it understands me. But then, time and again, I'm disappointed with it. How, for instance, can it choose the word for "nose" (*hana*), when I want to write "flower" (*hana*)? Both words look identical in the alphabet, but they are pronounced with different intonations and, of course, written with different ideograms. The computer isn't interested in what I write, but simply picks whichever symbol I have chosen previously. Not surprisingly, the computer writes "nose" because I use the word "nose" much more often than the word "flower." In classical eastern Asian literature the flower, next to the bird, the wind and the moon, is one of the four most important motifs in poetry, but since I'm more influenced by Nicolai Gogol's "Nose" than by the *Kokin Wakashū* or the like, the nose is more important to me than the flower. The computer also noticed it. It chose the symbol for "nose" when I wanted to thank a girlfriend for the flowers. "Thank you for the nose you've sent me." Some people say a computer doesn't understand context. But in this case, there was no context, as the e-mail consisted of only this very sentence. And what about the context outside the text? Is there any reason at all why I should never receive a nose as a present? It has happened that people have received cut-off body parts in their mail. Neither a context nor a writing program will protect us from it. What kind of writing system is a nose found in the breakfast roll based on? The question remains open. I describe it as "the nose of a nose." The Japanese word *nase*, pronounced with a short *a*, means "why," but in the alphabet is written exactly like the German word *Nase*.[2]   2. "Nose"

Hirnmaden
Brain Grubs

Our youngest child is of a quiet disposition, good at keeping silent and consequently also at developing thoughts we don't know from any of his older siblings. Hence he doesn't want to be himself sometimes.

It began with him wanting to have thick fur as well as claws and teeth, like the two bear cubs I found amid felled trees in the Taiga of the north, which I took home with me and kept for a few days before I handed them over to the state circus. A timidity toward the young bears, not much bigger than some shop teddy bears but already very predatory, never entirely left the children, who were allowed to live with them at a breath's distance. But then, as I was about to take them away for good, one under each arm, the youngest said all of a sudden: "Oh, how much I'd like to be a bear cub!"

Why, I want to know. Does he also want to leave?

No, not that. The reason is simpler: If he were one of them, he would never have been afraid and would have stood up to them.

He could still do it now, I try to persuade him.

No, the human child says resolutely, he would only do that if he were properly armed.

At that time he was five years old. Later on he also wanted to slip into a different skin now and again. At first into a rabbit's, then into the wolf's from the famous children's film "Just you wait!" He wants to be a sparrow, a mouse, a circus monkey from Vietnam and many others, human beings too: a cosmonaut, a girl, an aged person. Grandmother, for instance.

He wants to be the rabbit so, as he puts it, he can enjoy the affection of people. The wolf in order to shed its wickedness and thus save it, the actually very beautiful and mighty creature, from itself. The sparrow, to wean it from the filth of the street, the tiny red monkey to find out whether it knew that it delighted its own descendants with its pranks. The cosmonaut was to reveal how he felt seeing himself all the time: on the street, in the newspapers, on television, in the movies, in school books, even on the lapels of many children and adults, even of teachers, who are otherwise so strict and keen to reprimand.

Lately he wants to be two children from his class at the same time. One of them has a party and state leader for a father and a minister for a mother. The father is driven in a black Volga,[1] the mother in a white one. One of the cars takes the child to school in the morning, the other picks it up in the afternoon. Once, he says, both cars came at the same time. The other child's mother is a cleaning woman and his father died a few months ago.

1. A Russian car often used for governmental or business purposes

"Why two people at the same time? It's even more impossible!" I point out to him.

"Of course such a thing is impossible. But still it would be nice if it were possible!" he insists. "Then I could live with my one half here and with the other there. To see, to listen to two things at the same time, to drink from two bowls, to eat from two plates, to walk with one foot and to sit in the driving car with the other, letting it dangle in sheer boredom from the sparkling-clean, soft seat. Wouldn't you also like to do that, Father?"

I admit, I would like to do it. But then the adult in me stirs again and I say: "You've got strange wishes, child. Perhaps you don't like being with us very much, don't really want to be our nestling?"

The child, unjustly treated, flares up: "How can you say that, Father? I'm happy to be here, happy to be your child! I just want to know how it is with others, that's all!" Later he adds, now in his considerate way again: "Had I been another, then I most certainly would have wished to be what I am here."

Today, the boy, still a child and more than ever our youngest, studies in eighth grade. Here is a passage from an essay he wrote: "The residence of a pupil lies between the sand hill of yes and the stone hill of no. The adults, who create this kind of geography and guard over its sanctity, must have lived elsewhere when they were children. Because this place seems difficult to inhabit, and someone who doesn't have a choice but to stay there can easily get strange thoughts. I call them brain grubs . . ."

Galsan Tschinag

After almost a thousand days and nights I arrive again in this corner of my homeland and half of the clan rushes from all sides even before the dust trail of the mail van that has dropped me here at the edge of the Ail can settle. In the front of this swarm of people surging toward me are of course the children, and just at the moment when the first of them has reached me, a boy stumbles and falls face-forward into dust and dirt and remains sprawled out on the ground. Worried, I rush toward him and when the little stumbler, whose face, with beaming eyes and his mouth twisted in pain, resembling a shred of creased earth, becomes aware of my presence, he overcomes himself and exclaims with the last of his strength: "*Mys men*—am a cat!" and with the agility of a cat he takes off on all fours.

When the last leaves are falling from the urban aspen trees and the tepid yellow autumn winds give way to the winter grey and the snowstorms, life, even in the capital, becomes much more difficult. Many goods are getting scarcer and the queues longer. The search begins. Like that for milk. You may have money, or you may have time, or you may have money and time and a jug and a lot of other things, but it is hard, hard, hard to find milk if your mother or wife or girlfriend isn't a saleswoman or at least a cleaning woman in a grocery store.

In one such milk-scarce time I enter a shop with an empty jug and my negative attitude toward the socialist supply system, and I can't believe my eyes: milk is available! So I hurriedly join in, ready to participate in the battle of the queue. Yet, shortly after it is announced that the milk has run out!

"Run out" here means "*nichts mehr*" in German, "nonexistent" in science, "no horse is fast enough to catch up with the illusive" in the proverb—and for my mother, who had just been visiting, black tea, upset stomach and departure . . .

The queue slowly disperses; still, we, the cheated, cannot leave right away. And so we linger, undecided, like people who have been stood up.

Then two blue-smocked women, both cleaners, come rushing in from different sides and they set upon their higher-ranking colleague, the saleswoman, not much different from two dogs attacking a wolf. Throw at her all the expressions from the newspapers, call her an impudent, greedy person who lets everything disappear through the back door, a pernicious, petit-bourgeois element who has long deserved to be removed from the socialist cooperative.

The attacked, however, carries herself rather un-wolfishly, patiently endures the double-barrelled scolding while she silently busies herself with the empty containers. Then she rubs her backside against a forty-litre jug, winking with one eye in the process. Everyone understands: This one is still full.

Only the two comrades-in-arms fail to notice the furtive signal and the clamour continues. Until a man from the on-looking and eavesdropping crowd steps up to the furies and speaks to them quietly: "But she is letting you know that there is still milk in that one jug!"

One of the naggers understands immediately, nudges the other, whereupon even she finely becomes silent. But then the quicker of the two blue smocks casts a contemptuous glance at the informant and hisses at him in an undertone, so that it can only be heard by the one who until then had been condemned. But now it goes: "And, so what? *She* is the saleswoman and she is entitled to put aside a jar for the working staff of the house!"

And with this she disappears, pulling along her colleague by the hand, around the next corner.

Once again the tenured professor and I quarrel, that is, he raves and indulges me with extra-academic expressions and all of this in a rather un-professorial volume and I sit down, lean back, keep silent and stare with a fixed gaze at his defective eye and think to myself: If I were a raven, I would think twice before pecking my beak into this ugliness of a face!

That I, his subordinate, should be taking this liberty while keeping the right corner of my mouth in a continuous grin is getting too much for him: All of a sudden he clenches his right fist, bangs against the desk top and bellows: "Miserable wretch!"

And in that fraction of a second, as banging and bellowing collide, the door opens and in comes the dean. My vis-à-vis straightens his face, slowly bends toward me and says, so that it is clearly audible to the other: "This, or in a similar fashion, is how many teachers behave and thus lose the respect of the students. As a young teacher you ought to remember this!" Whereupon he extends a fatherly glance at me and turns with a sorrowful but assiduous face to his superior.

Auf der Heimreise
On the Way Home

I'm singing. I'm doing it again as I used to in the past, I'm singing about the slender white birch that is waiting for someone in summer and winter, and about the heart-warming love that lives in an inseparable, indefinable bond with the birch.

I'm singing with Russian girls in felt boots and padded pants. Snow lies on the ground, larch and birch forest stand all around us, and high above a water-blue sky is glistening, undulating.

Bells are ringing out from somewhere. One of the girls strikes up the song about those famous silver chimes, the others join in, it grows into a grand chorus.

A horse and cart approaches from behind. It is a sledge loaded with hay. A bell dangles and jingles at the horse's neck, and a little old man looks out of from the hay. He holds the reigns tightly, has a stern, as if put-on face, and calls out loudly: "Hey, my beauties, will you kindly make way!" The voice sounds oddly brisk, contains suppressed kindness and the slight, forgivable vanity of men advanced in years wanting to appear youthfully bold.

The girls have a good ear, they play at being offended and call back: "We are singing a song for you and you want to chase us off the road?"

An ashamed reply comes quickly in return: "Never mind, my darlings. Keep on singing and learn how to take a joke!" We are singing the song to the end. The sledge has not overtaken us. The reigns in his hands are not pulled so tightly anymore. The horse ambles unhurriedly, its head slightly drooping, just as the driver's.

"We sang the most beautiful of songs for you, now you'll have to let us stay at your place!" It resounds from the bevy of girls.

The reply comes quickly, the voice still as brisk as before: "And what if my bride gets jealous?"

"Your old lady better tell us how we can hold back our prince who wants to leave us!"

"Oho, and you've also got a prince with you? Where are you from, and where are you headed, you and your prince?"

"It's true, we've got a prince in our midst who has accompanied us over many mountains and rivers and now wants to vanish behind many mountains and rivers. We come from the town of Bijsk, we're apprentices there, want to learn how to take care of animals in your *dnejka*."

"But how come you, from the town of Bijsk, and your prince from even farther away, travel on foot to our *dnejka*?"

"It's because there are no planes or trains travelling to you, and our driver thought that there are no policemen either in these parts. Our luggage and our old man are waiting for the driver to sleep it off, but we didn't want to wait any longer and set off on foot to your *dnejka*."

"Then you're very welcome in our *dnejka*! Since there's not enough room for all of you in the hay I have to hurry on alone and get the village ready for the arrival of our guests, giddy-up!"

At last the girls let the horse sledge pass and strike up a song about the troika dashing off. Later they also sing about frost-wind and snow-dust, about arrivals and farewells, and about the prince, who wandered about in distant lands searching for happiness. I sing along although I'm hearing half of the songs for the first time, I'm lightheaded and at the same time seized by a faint sorrow, like a real prince.

We arrive at dusk. From a dozen tiny chimneys above the wooden huts it's smoking as if in competition. A motley crew of dogs and children rushes noisily toward us. People come out of their huts and stand waiting. Cows are mooing. Bells clang.

The children have taken our hands and we already know all of their names and what they can do by the time we stand in front of the waiting villagers. We recognize our friend among them; a tall, plump woman stands at his side, not old at all, with red glowing cheeks. She throws her arms wide open and laughs from the top of her voice, "Yes, I see, I'm going to have a fit of jealousy!" It smells of fresh bread, birchwood and stables.

I think about the home I left an eternity ago and am hurrying back to now. I think about the fairy tale of my life and feel a burning desire to fall into the arms of the people gathered here and to press my face into the coarse and tender palm of one of these Russian mothers. I think about the fairy tale of humankind, of its small and quiet and its great and loud achievements, think about how much human be-ings, however far apart, essentially resemble one another.

I think about the German girl Ursula, who was always seeking out differences, and devotedly represented a small part of the world she believed to be centuries ahead of mine, only to experience the sun, the moon, the million stars every day with the eternal six-hour delay. I think about her grey and tired town of Doberlug-Kirchhain, about her quiet, overloaded house on the Elster river and her curious readi-ness to pursue the affairs of an orderly life with tame diligence. I think about something that didn't happen but could have happened.

It is a beautiful, magnificent evening. It is followed by a strange night. No one really sleeps. It is simply a shame to be sleeping. I'm delighted and pained by the desire to press my heart into the hand of one of the Russian girls in felt boots and padded pants. But I know that I mustn't as I have to move on in the morning and I don't want to light a futureless fire in a heart that sooner or later would belong to someone else.

Feridun Zaimoglu

FÜNF KLOPFENDE HERZEN, WENN DIE LIEBE SPRINGT
FIVE BEATING HEARTS, WHEN LOVE LEAPS

During the high season of resistance I relied on a woman. I still had thirty-eight full days to live and then, regardless of a possible turn for the better, I simply wanted to commit suicide according to plan. I knew how to cut my wrists, I knew the short way to death. In my mind I had gone over an accident I knew from other scenarios; not until their fourth beer did the boys dare to talk about how their beautiful, dolled-up, immaculate dream girls had lost it, and the boys had to behave impeccably, a huge sense of guilt was burning them out, transforming them into horribly frosty whiners. I didn't know how they felt but I listened to them just the same. This best describes the state I was in at that time: an acquaintance, a friend, or a stranger would ramble on to himself and I'd be the confidant, now and again I'd be asked for an opinion and I'd volunteer an idle remark. I hadn't really finished with life yet, and every day I swallowed vitamin and calcium pills, went to the baker and newsagent, sat at the desk and wrote short stories I didn't have to be ashamed of. My fingers moved on and above the keyboard and when it clicked I knew it was time I cut my fingernails. I hate the slimy white of dusk, definitely bright and definitely dark are my favourite colours and that's why I leave the house at midday and at night. At that time, however, I was less scrupulous, I left my flat whenever I felt like it. I knew each day was getting me closer to my final goal, soon I would have reached the finishing line and I would at last step out of this community of waxed and sulphured people, of finance optimisers and their one hundred percent capital guarantee; I thought, get out of this bourgeois world that lays siege to me and us, I actually thought: fuck it, beat them to it, take yourself out before the final date they've set for you arrives; finished, you no longer depend on them, you're no longer vulnerable, you are no longer. I didn't want to breathe sense into this rubblescape around me and therefore I didn't want to leave a goodbye note; my death was promised to me and I would seal it and in the meantime I wrote my stories, full stop.

I didn't kill myself, she stepped in. The thirty-eighth day before the end began promisingly: A bassoon trio played a heart-wrenchingly melancholic Slavic folk tune underneath my window and I paused for a moment getting dressed, the right leg already half way down my trousers and my hands at the waistband; the Russians played and it hit me for the first time that winter day. I was standing in the kitchen—half of my life took place here—and I saw the empty mineral water bottles, the plastic dish rack, the instant soup bags, I saw folders and files with messages and reminders from the tax office and the knick-knacks you keep and collect although you have no use for them. The more I work the more I get stuck in the pressures of the trade, I juggle from one deadline to the next and while other people get pissed, stoned, or fall in love, I sit on my arse and type page after page, and when the Turks in the flat above me kick up a row again, I get up, climb on a chair and bang on the ceiling with a broom handle. That's why my ex-girlfriend thought I was a spoilsport and cleared out at some stage and grabbed herself a jolly air-guitarist, a great guy with a triple-pierced tongue and a dragon's head on his biceps that he brought to life with muscle play. He is a permanent member of the scene in the Schanzenviertel.[1] Here in the Schanze a different set of rules applies than in the rest of Hamburg, at least that's what the newcomers from the provinces believe. But if you walk along Hauptstraße, the main artery between Julius- and Eifflerstraße, you notice the unmistakable signs of gentrification that every leftist cultural milieu has coming: On the right side of the street fish restaurants take turns with Portuguese *Stehcafés*, gold jewellery boutiques and nostalgia furniture markets. The chic thirty-year-olds drink their Galao or Spanish red and watch the other side of the street, where you can choose between fighting for the next hit or the running battle against the existing wrong order. The junkies stand in front of the Fixstern, the technical personnel of the revolution live in the Rote Flora—my suspicious, agitated friends, who reproach me for having become middle class. I love them all the same because they do have a vague idea of how to succeed in breathing freely within a week without yoga and esoteric claptrap: An advertising agency slave just has to stop babbling about the value chain and he'll be his own master again, a teen TV starlet simply needs to drop her boobs back

1. A neighbourhood in Hamburg.

into her cups and she'll be credible when she talks about the subtlety of women's power. I know I'm a romantic and if I have to justify myself for it I'll refer to my ex-girlfriend, a vegetarian with a craving for spaghetti carbonara. She soaked granulated soya mince in a broth, it swelled up, looked like mince meat, but tasted like meat substitute. She consumed it bravely, and chewed it noisily. Abstaining from beef mince didn't affect her chronically good humour, she was inspired by an idea and the idea agreed with her. I suspect that this is not a plausible example, but that's exactly it—if you are sensitive and romantic you're always off the mark.

I managed to rouse myself and slip into my trousers, the Russian musicians moved on, even in my neighbourhood people dislike spending time with street artists in the morning. The footpath was iced over, the snowploughs had shifted the snow from the street onto the curb, I trudged into furrows of brown slush, the water ran into my sneakers and before long I had wet feet. People were queuing in front of the three ATMs of the *Sparkasse*, Gerd sat in his sleeping bag under the bank's awning and asked for fifty cents or a cigarette. Had I not turned to him and raised my arm in greeting I could have just avoided the Mini Cooper that shot out of a parking gap, and the woman at the wheel, seething with rage at that moment, would have accelerated instead of hitting the break, given me the finger in the rear mirror with a loud beep, having had an excuse to vent her anger. Instead it hit me for the second time that day, she got me with the mudguard actually, a heavy blow from the side. I went down and sat in the slush, I remember how I groped in the dirty snow between my legs as if I couldn't believe it, and then she sat next to me and I gaped at her legs and thought she shouldn't do this, she'll catch a terrible cold. Then I lifted my head and looked at her, I saw her talking, but her words didn't get through to me, she had wonderful green-blue eyes. Suddenly the buzzing in my ears faded and I was able to understand her, she was worried and, strangely, felt me over for possible fractures; I said that I felt no pain, I said she could walk me to the first floor of the yellow house over there, and while she helped me to get up and the ice-water ran from my trouser bottoms, I decided not to shake off the shock in a hurry. I wanted her to stay for an hour because by that time, at the very latest, I would have fallen in love.

I fell in love with her because she almost died of worry and expected the very worst: A great assassin she would have made. I sent her straight back down to the street, drug related crime and traffic wardens are on the prowl around the clock and an unlocked, double-parked vehicle is easy prey. My trousers were heavy and wet and sticking to my skin, I was freezing miserably, so I got changed in the kitchen. The woollen socks got caught in the hem of my trousers, I bent over, breathing heavily, and clumsily pulled at them. Suddenly the door swung open. At the sight of my naked behind raised like a duck's arse she burst out laughing. She laughed like I hadn't heard a woman laugh before and I fled into the bathroom, both hands covering my sex and the damned trousers at my ankles. When I returned and asked if I could offer her an instant coffee, she started again and I had a broad grin on my face because she really shook with laughter; her hair got messed up and stuck out on all sides, and the flush on her cheeks was remarkable. Although I didn't mention it, she told me that as a child she had liked being out in the cold and once, when she was five and sitting on a sledge pulled by her father, her face had become frozen, and she got apple cheeks ever since, even at inopportune moments. For the last and third time it hit me that day; my heart was in flames; this is the whole and simple truth. She wasn't nosey, she didn't ask questions, she pointed to the deer's-head magnet on the fridge door; she also had deer on her pin board and their antlers had also broken off, by and by, they looked like fat antelopes. Then she wanted to know whether the thing on the floor was a desk vacuum cleaner, and I told her that Gerd, the young homeless guy from around the corner, traded in abstruse consumer objects, apart from his main occupation as a scrounger; where he obtained them remained a mystery, and that thing by the way was a steam cleaning jet, which blasted calcium deposits off bathroom fittings. She had another laughing fit and I couldn't take my eyes off her. Intrigued by the police sirens I walked to the window, the riots had been scheduled for late that night; surely the undercover cops were mingling with the people, eavesdropping on discussions and passing on the latest rumours to headquarters. Yesterday a friend of the Rote Flora, an anarcho-syndicalist, talked about the impending collision of the contingents and he called the increased police presence in the Schanze a provocation. I turned around and asked her name. Lulu she said, and yours? Fernando I said, I swear, it's my Christian name. We remained quiet for a moment and thought about these names, Lulu and Fernando, it didn't sound worse than Frieda and Karl-Johann. By now I felt the pain on my left side; I was going to get big black bruises; I couldn't think of anything interesting to say. She looked at her wrist-watch, a Gucci imitation, got up and said she owed me, I had to come to the Eisenstein in Altona, she was waitressing there and would shout me a pizza of my choice. See you later, I called after her—she had stayed for almost an hour and it had been long enough, I sucked in the air, her perfume tickled my nose.

There's trouble in the air, the bourgeois say, where the revolutionaries have barricaded and fenced themselves off, the state authorities and their baton-armed troops have to intervene and close up, plug the holes, not an inch for the rats, it's even written in the *Feuilleton*. It all began when two cops on patrol issued a red card to a derelict who couldn't handle it because he didn't permit outsiders to invade his system. The vagrant was not of this world anymore: every few steps he came to a halt and bowed to an imaginary power. He refused everyone access to his imaginings, only once had I ever seen him sitting on the front steps of a house entrance engaging in civilized conversation with a friend from the Flora. An insane *Lumpen*-rastafari in his small world of obsessions. He didn't hurt anyone and there was no one wanting to chase him just because he stopped at the wrong place. Sometimes the Bible enthusiasts from the Spiritueller Shop looked after him, they gave him bread and water, but they couldn't lure him into their place of worship. On the afternoon in question the cops blocked his path, they asked him for his ID and when he didn't react they told him to move on and because the unapproachable man didn't want to stop his kowtows, they thought he was making fun of them and they shoved him, or rather, they shook him and he fell. They surrounded the lunatic on the ground, he screamed, as anyone would in anticipation of an impending injury; in fact, later on he had to be treated for a broken wrist. The cops were about to leave, but before they knew it they were surrounded by outraged *Rotfloristen*, one word led to another, "pigs" rang out, they were called "henchmen" and warned to piss off or they'd get a hiding. Soon after, patrol cars arrived with their blue lights flashing and the mob dispersed, a few were apprehended and taken in for questioning. Reprisals were announced for the coming days, the henchmen would be met head-on, the mercenaries, as they were referred to, had mowed down a poor lunatic, and cowards don't go to heaven, the Bible enthusiasts said, because we all were and are in it together, the evangelists, the Rotflorians, the passers-by and the restaurateurs. And where was I at that time? I was lying on my mattress contemplating my suicide and then I got up and, as so often, stood at the window. I noticed the people who were all looking in one direction, and I even saw the Floristen stepping out from the side entrance, I could see that a state of emergency was about to unfold again, and it's always just a small step from emergency to escalation, the wires run hot and in the end the black-hooded faction, who are deeply convinced that this peace is a rotten one, are proven right. From my crow's nest I looked down on the witnesses of an escalating situation, I wanted no more than the warmth of the room and the typewriter in the back. I thought: He who gets involved will suffer. That's how I am.

I had a lot of time to kill before evening. I didn't write anything, not a single word. A budding love, a love you don't even know you feel, is like a fainting fit, no, a series of fits, and the minutes in between contort beyond measure, as if staring at the hour hand and waiting until it finally cuts across the next stroke. I didn't want to stare at the clock forever, and even though it was sleeting heavily and tiny hailstones pelted against the windows I got going, where to, remained to be seen. In those days I had long hair, thick strands limited my field of vision—to look sideways I had to turn my head and since I disliked moving my head it was easy to attack me from the side. I enjoyed that bit of danger. The wall posters of the Rote Flora called for battle, a riot-weary resident had scribbled underneath that he figured that, because of a great TV program and the bad weather, the slimeballs wouldn't leave their digital squares. I left my flat, I left my neighbourhood, I left my people, I held the open umbrella at an angle against the wind, my neck was unprotected and exposed to the rain, a wonderful feeling. I walked and paused, I stood at a red light and read an advertising leaflet stuck at eye level from a jewellery workshop that invited you to a dance with a fairy; I watched a puppy trying vainly to catch a wind-whirled leaf with its snout. A trophy shop was offering all kinds of engravings, club gear and football fan paraphernalia. I bumped into unknown people and I didn't care because so many things lay beyond my reach, I was almost proud about keeping my mouth shut and harbouring twisted thoughts. Eventually it seemed unimportant to wait for the right moment, and so, after a long forced march, I walked into the Zeisenhallen. I went into the Eisenstein, sat at the first available table, looked at and saw her, I saw only her, there was no other in this large hall than Lulu. She appeared baffled to see me again so soon, she was just wrapping the white waitress's apron around her waist and looked like an actress changing for her role. She talked briefly to the two Africans behind the pizza counter then came to my table and, before I could launch into an explanation, asked me to join her for a cigarette in the courtyard. She had five minutes, she couldn't look after me, I should go and see a doctor, please. The sheen on her eyelids was indescribable. Her long fingers, running into almost dainty fingertips, were indescribable. She inhaled deeply; she had been angry and her anger had clouded her vision, usually she only drove in a sober frame of mind—I liked her somewhat old-fashioned diction. And since I didn't ask who or what had provoked her anger, she told me two long drags later that her best friend had become pregnant to a married man and she wanted the child and a different life as a young mother. She dropped the cigarette, stubbed it out with her fake snake leather stiletto heels. We went back inside again, the ribbons of her apron bobbed with each step. I was about to return to my table but she introduced the Africans first, they were called Gottfried one and two, ultra-serious Ghanaians in white T-shirts and white pants. They were spreading sauce over the rolled-out pizza base, and a certain Darius, a not very kosher ethnic German emigrant, was responsible for the pizza dough. When his face moved it looked like hardening wax.

I slid back through a group of musical-goers and immersed myself in the menu. Barbarie duck, rack of lamb and boar: I was, to use Lulu's words, in much too sober a frame of mind to ruin my stomach with it. And then she stood next to me all of a sudden and drew out a pencil stub, moistening its tip like a book-keeper. I almost lost control at the sight of her but composedly ordered a Quattro Stagioni and didn't understand why she cracked up, her centre of gravity buckled below her navel and she shook with laughter. After she had calmed down a little she revealed to me that the Hanseatic philistine made a virtue out of his indecisiveness and ordered the "multi-topping pizza": one quarter each of artichoke, salami, ham and mushrooms. At least I hadn't, like the worst of the philistines, chosen a crispy spinach dough with egg in the middle. She stood and I sat and because I'm old-fashioned in these matters I got up and said, Soon I'll be strong enough to chase away your troubles—only, of course, if you let me. Lulu took a good look at me, it almost felt as if she was studying my face. I've got a headache, she said, and I asked her to wait and not to go anywhere. I stormed out of the Eisenstein, running so fast that my heels drummed against my butt, and eventually found a Turkish corner shop, where I purchased a half-litre bottle of raki and ten ginger roots, placed a twenty euro bill on the counter and didn't wait for the change. Less than ten minutes later I was back again—she was just about to serve my philistine pizza—and I instructed her to put as many ginger roots as possible into the schnapps and in half an hour I would begin with the treatment of her headache. She smiled, she didn't laugh, she smiled. Meanwhile all the tables had been taken, even at the side table next to the coat rack there were three couples sitting squeezed together with their elbows pulled in. The patrons consisted of the upper cultural stratum, the typical pop and porno models of a city, the bourgeoisie and their toddlers clad in frilled skirts and ironed jeans. A pale young poet coughed pretentiously into his hand and his girlfriend couldn't think of anything better to do than to pick her paper serviette to pieces out of sheer boredom. I knew his poetry, he had composed a poem in which he describes how he or his alter ego puts up his legs on a disk relief cube made of foam and drinks apple juice. I plastered the wall above my bed with the fourteen pages of the poem, I can recite parts of it from memory, I wish it was I who composed it. Still, it would have been too daft to express my admiration openly, I was stuck on my chair and wondered, while eating my pizza, whether the thirty-eighth day before my unannounced suicide would take a turn for the better or the worse. Was she the woman of my life or did she have a boyfriend, a lover, a husband? A woman like her really ought to have a smart Italian on the leash. I shooed away the bad thoughts, and as if she had just been waiting for it, she turned up and said the half hour was over. I followed her to the courtyard, she turned over a tin bucket, put it on the ground and sat down, her eyes shut tight; the eyelashes twitched like a child's who dreams of low-flying birds, brushed by their shadows. I fished a couple of ginger roots out of the salad bowl and softly began to massage her temples in a circular motion. A few minutes later she opened her eyes again and said, now she knew my hands better than me and wasn't sure if she was willing to change anything about it. Her temples were flushed from the ginger massage and the flush also coloured her high, firm cheekbones, her cheeks, her neck. Without much shame I confessed to her that I was a novice in love and willing still to get into difficulties; I knew I was at an age where everything was possible or almost everything, and within a year I would begin to judge people by the distances they kept between themselves and companions from the past, and soon perhaps I'd also claim, There's clutter behind me and prostheses in front. She didn't understand a word, her face between the rotating ginger roots just beamed at me and I stopped short in the middle of my poetic rubbish and asked her permission to pick her up after her shift. She said she had to haul pizzas until two, and out of joy I bit into the ginger root and took a big gulp out of the salad bowl.

I was caught by the main current, I drifted off the edge of the embankment and only just managed to keep my head above water. Or to put it more simply: I was touched by a woman, I thought she was an apparition, an inexplicable phenomenon, and although I pinched my skin her beauty didn't disappear. Or more mystically: The she-wolf sensed me on her hunting spree and when I offered her my throat she bared her fangs and I did likewise. Or more problematically: We talked and talked and talked, but still she saw no common ground for love, she couldn't give a damn about a man . . .

While walking back to my neighbourhood in the sleet, I pictured uncertain outcomes, bad endings and, in between, fables of salvation. I was clearly out of my mind. For the first time in a long while I felt truly alive and aware, because usually I remained passive in good and bad situations alike as I knew they could always be rewritten as a story. I had enough of being a spectator, half a day had been sufficient to transform me from the occasional walk-on to a potential lover. I didn't look through a strong lens anymore for the pictures to fit together to a snapshot. If you're in love you're inclined to self-deception, it may be true—but that's how I wanted it and not any different.

In the Schulterblatt I met with small units, groups of five to ten people, Floristen and sympathizers fervently awaiting the eruption, calling upon me, their half-comrade, to join them. There would be an explosion, that much was certain. In front of the bare ivy on the facade of a Flora wing a few hooded activists warmed their hands at flames flickering out of a metal drum. A vagrant passed by, he was given a place at the fire. Ever more people streamed into the neighbourhood reporting that police vans with sirens and blue lights were on their way; the water cannons were being kept in the background—they would advance if the cops encountered a stronger than expected resistance. They would be given a great welcome because, from our point of view, it was they who were the hooligans, pub brawlers in stupid uniforms, and the women among these thugs clobbered especially hard—with the truncheon in their hand they were the creatures of men and would remain so. For the cops it was also simple—they waged war against wogs, schmucks and lefties, the truncheon always hit the right one, and afterward they sold it as restoring law and order. Tonight, I thought, it could work, it could be different, and in my excitement I went from one group to the next, aware that I was acting like an undercover cop collecting material for his latest report. The fire from the oil drum drew silhouettes on the cobblestones of figures moving up and down, a crush as if a tribe was gathering, keeping a night vigil in front of a ruin, its surrender out of the question. I had to leave right now, later it would be impossible to get behind the lines, behind the police cordon. And I turned away, perhaps it was shabby, perhaps they, my half-comrades, would justly reproach me for being a riot tourist who clears out as soon as it gets dicey. How could I talk to them about my love? The private isn't political, sometimes it is in the way of political action. I wasn't alone, to be sure, with my vague aversion against everything to do with being victorious—but to miss a confrontation because you want to pick up a woman is going too far.

Only two blocks farther down the cops got out of the police vans, the body armour underneath their uniform making them look like angular gladiators. The squad leader radioed the coordinates. When I saw the plexiglass shields I knew they would seal their ranks and advance with great speed and the running wall would clear away everything that hadn't moved out of its path in time. A few men sat on the cast-iron grid around a lone elm tree and strapped perforated protective pads on their thighs, a bulky giant braced himself against a concrete bollard and put on his helmet. It was the time shortly before the collision, on the other side my friends would also be gearing up for it . . .

She waited for me in front of the archway of the Zeisehallen and watched me as I came closer, and perhaps she noticed my growing insecurity, I didn't want to scare her off with a kiss on the mouth but I was dying to cover her face in kisses. She gave me a kiss on the lips and softly pushed me away, the lights of the hall extinguishing behind her. The sky had poured itself out and a blunt mother-of-pearl stirred up the cold winter blue, the shimmer of the ice made the streets look like fable paths; here and there, like stripes of soot on skin, rubber trace of tires. A premature word would have ruined everything, she, quietly exhaling clouds of breath, would have disappeared without a promise to see me again. She was exhausted and she entrusted herself to me; perhaps she left the decision up to me; I felt bliss knowing her so close and would have loved to tell her, Lulu, you're my happiness, and what a truly wonderful woman you are. In a good manners guide I had read that the rule to follow the woman doesn't apply when entering coffee-houses. When we were standing in front of the Greenwich bar I pulled the door's handlebar with both hands and

held the door open for her regardless. Behind the long bar counter
Gio was drying cocktail glasses and when he saw me he clicked his
tongue, mimicking some gunslinger from an Italo-Western. I caught
up with Lulu and we walked up the stairs to the so-called lounge area,
a bench ran along the length and breadth of the wall, a few dollhouse
tables and chairs were arranged in parallel. The ashtrays were sunk
into wooden cubes, and the downlights set in jet housings produced
a half-light that seemed perfectly adjusted to the harsh melancholia
of the patrons. A minimalist suicide jazz was playing, the type of music that inevitably made you think of coke and wasted musicians. The
pretentious ambience got on my nerves, Lulu smoked silently and
let her gaze wander, a tired night owl on her last short public appearance. We both ordered beer. After her first sip she said without turning her face to me, it was funny somehow that the man she'd almost
run over first massaged her with ginger roots and then took her out, as
if to thank her for it. Then she laughed again, the men and women at
the other tables and on the bench interrupted their conversations and
looked at her, she laughed and shook off her tiredness. And then she
said she absolutely had to pull out this one hair from my ear lobe now,
her fingers were itching, and the next moment I felt a sting and was
a little embarrassed in front of the gawkers. If this continued I would
suffer more bruises and bleeding pores. I know this is happening too
fast, I said, and you should take your time, but one should love and
be loved before it is too late. I felt a strong desire to talk myself into
trouble, an eruption from the heart without filter or muffler flowing
out of me, but Lulu put her fingers on my lips, kissed the back of her
hand, a long, chaste kiss. We let go of each other, the clock on a col-
umn showed quarter past three, it was time to leave. A guy in his mid-
twenties approached her; he was fitted with a retro suit, purple check-
ers on beige background, and repeatedly ran his fingers through his
hair and adjusted the fringe on his forehead. It turned out that they
knew each other from a holiday in Mallorca, ten years ago yet unfor-
gotten; in those days it had been possible, in those days Mallorca had
not been German territory. I stood close by but wasn't introduced.
Suddenly the boy said, I actually thought you were dead. A woman
had told him, Max's sister to be precise, you know, he said, Max, your

great love. Lulu turned her back and headed for the exit, I crumpled up a ten euro note and threw it in Gio's direction, he loved cinematic scenes. Lulu was waiting across the street and I had a sense of déjà vu, I rushed over, slipped and just caught my balance, or rather she grabbed my arm and I steadied myself. We'll do it differently, she said, I'll walk you home, I hate gentlemen.

I dislike walking actually, but for her sake I would have somersaulted all the way back to the Schanze. I said, when I was trying to perform a halfway decent hand spring in year seven I landed so awkwardly that I had to wear a brace around my crooked neck for two weeks. Lulu didn't laugh and I blushed in the dark. I'm not dead, she said, I'm still alive, and . . . Max, yes, my great love back then, the relationship was nothing but a dead communication channel, I just couldn't get away from him, I think you know what I mean. I didn't know, I just wrote stories about men and women.

The closer we came to my neighbourhood, the harder it was for me to comfort her with mere words; most of the past is irrelevant and a Max whose name might be Maximillian and was punished for life didn't matter, at least not any more than before the accident in the morning. The lovers of old, wrapped in black brocade, caringly forgotten and left behind, were stirring again, they seldom remained in the artificial darkness under heavy cloth, they emerged sooner or later, one wrongly believed oneself to be safe. A wrong move, a wrong touch, a wrong word—all of a sudden I saw myself as a competitor, doomed to failure, how could I possibly stand up to a great love? I breathed out and looked up, a fire illuminated the sky above the Schanze and Lulu glanced into the distance, her view lost in the vanishing point of the housing rows. Your place is burning, she said, and smiled at me, her beautiful face close to my face. I can't be missing, I said, I'll have to be there, and she said, I know, I'll come with you. We would lose, no barricade and no hideout would protect us, and at the end of the small battle, we'd be ashamed of the fear we felt from the very first minute of our riot. We made the right decision: What else could we have done?

CARMEN-FRANCESCA BANCIU was born in 1955 in Lipova, Romania, and grew up in Arad and Timisoara. Between 1974 and 1980, she studied Christian art and foreign trade in Bucharest. After the fall of the socialist system, she migrated to Berlin where she currently lives with her children. "Flowers for Mother" is a translation of the first chapter of her novel *Das Lied der traurigen Mutter* published by Rotbuch Verlag in 2007.

Born in 1968 as the son of a German Polish parents, ARTUR BECKER grew up in Masuria, Poland. In 1985, the family migrated to West Germany where he studied Eastern European cultural history and German literature. He writes novels, short stories, poems, and essays and also works as a translator. "Kobra" is taken from *Milchstraße*, a short-story collection published in 2002 by Hofmann und Campe Verlag.

Until the age of ten, MARICA BODROŽIĆ lived with her grandfather in Sbvib, Dalmatia, Yugoslavia. In 1983, she moved to her *Gastarbeiter* parents in Germany and began to learn German. She studied anthropology, psychoanalysis and Slavic studies in Frankfurt am Main and in 2002, published her first short-story collection, *Tito ist tot*, where the two texts in this anthology originate, with Suhrkamp Verlag. She lives as a writer in Berlin.

DIMITRÉ DINEV was born in Plovdiv, Bulgaria, in 1968. In 1990, he fled to Austria across the "green border" and settled in Vienna, where he studied philosophy and Russian philology. The short-story collection *Licht über dem Kopf*, the title story of which is included in this anthology, was published in 2005 by Deuticke, in Vienna, where Dinev lives as a writer.

Born in 1946 in Budapest, ZSUZSANNA GAHSE fled Hungary with her parents in 1956. She went to school in Vienna and Kassel, Germany, and lived for over twenty years in Stuttgart. Since 1998, she has lived in Switzerland. *Instabile Texte zu zweit*, from which the present texts are taken, was published by Edition Korrespondenzen, Vienna, in 2005.

Luo Lingyuan was born in 1963 in the People's Republic of China. She studied computer science and journalism in Shanghai andand has lived in Berlin since 1980. Since 1992, she has been publishing in Chinese and German. The stories in this anthology originally appeared in her first volume of short stories, *Du fliegst jetzt für meinen Sohn aus dem fünften Stock!* Deutscher Taschenbuch Verlag, 2005.

Sudabeh Mohafez was born to a German mother and Iranian father in 1963. In 1979, the family moved from Teheran to Berlin. Mohafez studied music, English, and pedagogy and worked for many years as a social worker in a women's refuge. The stories in this anthology are from *Wüstenhimmel Sternenland*, which was published by Arche Zürich in 2004. At present, Mohafez lives in Stuttgart.

Terézia Mora was born in Sopron, Hungary in 1971 and moved to Berlin in 1990 where she studied Hungarian and performing arts. After her studies she trained as a scriptwriter at the Deutsche Film- und Fernsehakademie. Since 1998 she's worked as a freelance writer and translator. *Seltsame Materie*, whose title story is included in this anthology, was her first short-story collection, and was published by Rowohlt Verlag in 2000.

Herta Müller was born and grew up in an ethnic German village in the Banat region of Romania. She studied German and Romanian philology in Timisoara and later worked as a technical translator. Her first novel *Niederungen*, was published in a censored edition in 1982, and ongoing difficulties with the Ceauscesu regime led to her migration to West Berlin in 1987. Müller received numerous prizes and awards for her work and, in 2009, won the Nobel Prize for Literature. "There Are Different Eyes Inside Each Language" was first collected in her book of essays, *Der König verneigt sich und tötet*, published by Hanser Verlag in 2003.

Born in Malatya, Turkey, in 1946, EMINE SEVGI ÖZDAMAR first travelled to Berlin in 1965 where she stayed for two years, worked in a factory and learned German. She studied acting between 1967 and 1970 in Istanbul and returned to Berlin for an internship at the East Berlin *Volksbühne* in 1976. From 1979 to 1984, she worked as an actress at the *Bochumer Schauspielhaus*. Since 1986, she has been a freelance writer, living in Berlin. The original of "Mother Tongue" was published in *Mutterzunge* by Rotbuch Verlag in 1990 and reissued in 2010.

ILMA RAKUSA was born in Slovakia in 1946 and grew up in Budapest, Ljubljana, Triest and Zürich. She writes poetry and prose, works as a translator and academic and lives in Zürich. The prose collection *Durch Schnee*, from which the present stories were taken, was published by Suhrkamp Verlag in 2006.

YOKO TAWADA was born in Tokyo in 1960. She studied literature at Waseda University and in 1982, moved to Hamburg where she continued her studies in German literature. At that time, she began publishing prose and poetry in Japanese and German. In 1987, she received her doctorate at the University of Zürich, Switzerland. She currently lives in Berlin. The three prose pieces translated here originally appeared in the prose collection *Überseezungen*, published by Konkursbuch Verlag Tübingen in 2002.

The son of a Tuvan shaman, GALSAN TSCHINAG was born in a yurt in the Altai Mountains in western Mongolia in 1943. Refusing a stipend to study in Moscow in 1962, he instead studied German language and literature at the Karl Marx University in Leipzig. In 1968, he returned to Mongolia and taught German at the National University of Mongolia. In 1981, his first book in German, *Eine tuwenische Geschichte und andere Erzählungen*, was published in East Berlin, and other publications followed: poetry, short stories and novels, most of them written in German. He lives with his family in Ulan Bator, Mongolia. The three prose pieces in the present translation were originally published by Unionsverlag in 2008 in a volume entitled *Auf der großen blauen Straße*.

FERIDUN ZAIMOGLU was born in Bolu, Turkey, in 1964, and grew up in Germany. He studied fine arts and medicine in Kiel where he still lives and works as a writer, artist, and journalist. The present story originated in his collection *Zwölf Gramm Glück* by Kiepenheuer & Witsch, Köln, in 2004.

Thanks are due to the below-named publishers and authors for their kind permission to translate and publish the stories and excerpts in this volume.

Carmen-Francesca Banciu: "Flowers for Mother," excerpt from the novel *Das Lied der traurigen Mutter* ©2007 by Rotbuch Verlag, Berlin.

Artur Becker: "Kobra," from *Milchstraße* ©2002 by Hofmann und Campe Verlag, Hamburg.

Marica Bodrožić: "Tito is Dead" and "The War Returnee," from *Tito ist tot* ©2002 by Suhrkamp Verlag, Frankfurt.

Dimitré Dinev: "A Light Above the Head," from *Licht über dem Kopf* ©2005 by Deuticke im Paul Zsolnay Verlag, Wien.

Zsuzsanna Gahse: "Short Unstable Locality Guide," "Pelican," and "Say Nothing," from *Instabile Texte zu zweit* ©2005 by Edition Korrespondenzen, Wien.

Luo Lingyuan: "A Tender Bamboo Shoot" and "The Lovers, the Police and the Burglar King," from *Du fliegst jetzt für meinen Sohn aus dem fünften Stock!* ©2005 by Luo Lingyuan.

Sudabeh Mohafez: "The Slow-motion Scream" and "Sediment" from *Wüstenhimmel Sternenland* ©2004, 2012 by Arche Literatur Verlag AG, Zürich–Hamburg.

Terézia Mora: "Strange Matter" from *Seltsame Materie* ©2000 by Rowohlt Verlag GmbH, Reinbek / Hamburg.

Herta Müller: "There Are Different Eyes Inside Each Language," excerpted from the essay *"In jeder Sprache sitzen andere Augen,"* from *Der König verneigt sich und tötet* ©2003 by Herta Müller.

Emine Sevgi Özdamar: "Mother Tongue," from *Mutterzunge* ©1990, 2010 by Rotbuch Verlag, Berlin.

Ilma Rakusa: "The Door to the Sea," "Through Snow," and "Summer" from *Durch Schnee* ©2006 by Suhrkamp Verlag, Frankfurt a. M.

Yoko Tawada: "An Empty Bottle," "Letter Music," and "The Apple and the Nose," from *Überseezungen* ©2002 by Konkursbuch Verlag, Tübingen.

Galsan Tschinag: "Brain Grubs," "Inspirations," and "On the Way Home," from *Auf der großen blauen Straße* ©2008 by Unionsverlag, Zürich.

Feridun Zaimoglu: "Five Beating Hearts, When Love Leaps," from *Zwölf Gramm Glück* ©2004 by Verlag Kiepenheuer & Witsch GmbH & Co. KG, Köln.

EDUARD STOKLOSINSKI was born and grew up near Stuttgart, Germany, and graduated from the University of Bremen in 1987. In 1990, he migrated to Sydney, Australia, where he currently resides. In 2004, he received an MA in research from the University of Sydney. In 2012, he was awarded a Doctor of Arts from the University of Sydney, School of Letters, Art and Media.

MICHAL AJVAZ, *The Golden Age.*
The Other City.
PIERRE ALBERT-BIROT, *Grabinoulor.*
YUZ ALESHKOVSKY, *Kangaroo.*
FELIPE ALFAU, *Chromos. Locos.*
IVAN ÂNGELO, *The Celebration.*
The Tower of Glass.
ANTÓNIO LOBO ANTUNES, *Knowledge of Hell.*
The Splendor of Portugal.
ALAIN ARIAS-MISSON, *Theatre of Incest.*
JOHN ASHBERY & JAMES SCHUYLER, *A Nest of Ninnies.*
ROBERT ASHLEY, *Perfect Lives.*
GABRIELA AVIGUR-ROTEM, *Heatwave and Crazy Birds.*
DJUNA BARNES, *Ladies Almanack.*
Ryder.
JOHN BARTH, *Letters. Sabbatical.*
DONALD BARTHELME, *The King.*
Paradise.
SVETISLAV BASARA, *Chinese Letter.*
MIQUEL BAUÇÀ, *The Siege in the Room.*
RENÉ BELLETTO, *Dying.*
MAREK BIENCZYK, *Transparency.*
ANDREI BITOV, *Pushkin House.*
ANDREJ BLATNIK, *You Do Understand.*
LOUIS PAUL BOON, *Chapel Road.*
My Little War.
Summer in Termuren.
ROGER BOYLAN, *Killoyle.*
IGNÁCIO DE LOYOLA BRANDÁO, *Zero.*
Anonymous Celebrity.
BONNIE BREMSER, *Troia: Mexican Memoirs.*
CHRISTINE BROOKE-ROSE, *Amalgamemnon.*
BRIGID BROPHY, *In Transit.*
GERALD L. BRUNS, *Modern Poetry and the Idea of Language.*
GABRIELLE BURTON, *Heartbreak Hotel.*
MICHEL BUTOR, *Degrees. Mobile.*

G. CABRERA INFANTE, *Infante's Inferno.*
Three Trapped Tigers.
ARNO CAMENISCH, *The Alp*
JULIETA CAMPOS, *The Fear of Losing Eurydice.*
ANNE CARSON, *Eros the Bittersweet.*
ORLY CASTEL-BLOOM, *Dolly City.*
LOUIS-FERDINAND CÉLINE, *North.*
Rigadoon.
Castle to Castle.
Conversations with Professor Y.
London Bridge.
Normance.
MARIE CHAIX, *The Laurels of Lake Constance.*
HUGO CHARTERIS, *The Tide Is Right.*
ERIC CHEVILLARD, *Demolishing Nisard.*
MARC CHOLODENKO, *Mordechai Schamz.*
JOSHUA COHEN, *Witz.*
EMILY HOLMES COLEMAN, *The Shutter of Snow.*
ROBERT COOVER, *A Night at the Movies.*
STANLEY CRAWFORD, *Log of the S.S.*
The Mrs Unguentine.
Some Instructions to My Wife.
S.D. CHROSTOWSKA, *Permission*
RENÉ CREVEL, *Putting My Foot in It.*
RALPH CUSACK, *Cadenza.*
NICHOLAS DELBANCO, *Sherbrookes.*
The Count of Concord.
NIGEL DENNIS, *Cards of Identity.*
PETER DIMOCK, *A Short Rhetoric for Leaving the Family.*
ARIEL DORFMAN, *Konfidenz.*
COLEMAN DOWELL, *Island People.*
Too Much Flesh and Jabez.
ARKADII DRAGOMOSHCHENKO, *Dust.*
RIKKI DUCORNET, *Phosphor in Dreamland.*
The Complete Butcher's Tales.
The Jade Cabinet.
The Fountains of Neptune.

WILLIAM EASTLAKE, *The Bamboo Bed.*
Castle Keep.
Lyric of the Circle Heart.

JEAN ECHENOZ, *Chopin's Move.*

STANLEY ELKIN, *A Bad Man.*
Criers and Kibitzers, Kibitzers and Criers.
The Dick Gibson Show.
The Franchiser.
The Living End.
Mrs. Ted Bliss.

FRANÇOIS EMMANUEL, *Invitation to a Voyage.*

SALVADOR ESPRIU, *Ariadne in the Grotesque Labyrinth.*

LESLIE A. FIEDLER, *Love and Death in the American Novel.*

JUAN FILLOY, *Op Oloop.*

ANDY FITCH, *Pop Poetics.*

GUSTAVE FLAUBERT, *Bouvard and Pécuchet.*

KASS FLEISHER, *Talking out of School.*

JON FOSSE, *Aliss at the Fire.*
Melancholy.

FORD MADOX FORD, *The March of Literature.*

MAX FRISCH, *I'm Not Stiller.*
Man in the Holocene.

CARLOS FUENTES, *Adam in Eden.*
Christopher Unborn.
Distant Relations.
Terra Nostra.
Where the Air Is Clear.

TAKEHIKO FUKUNAGA, *Flowers of Grass.*

WILLIAM GADDIS, JR., *The Recognitions.*

JANICE GALLOWAY, *Foreign Parts.*
The Trick Is to Keep Breathing.

WILLIAM H. GASS, *Cartesian Sonata and Other Novellas.*
The Tunnel. Willie Masters' Lonesome Wife.

GÉRARD GAVARRY, *Hoppla! 1 2 3.*

ETIENNE GILSON, *The Arts of the Beautiful.*
Forms and Substances in the Arts.

C. S. GISCOMBE, *Giscome Road.*
Here.

DOUGLAS GLOVER, *Bad News of the Heart.*

WITOLD GOMBROWICZ, *A Kind of Testament.*

PAULO EMÍLIO SALES GOMES, *P's Three Women.*

GEORGI GOSPODINOV, *Natural Novel.*

JUAN GOYTISOLO, *Count Julian.*
Juan the Landless.
Makbara.
Marks of Identity.

HENRY GREEN, *Back.*
Blindness.
Concluding.
Doting.
Nothing.

JACK GREEN, *Fire the Bastards!*

JIŘÍ GRUŠA, *The Questionnaire.*

MELA HARTWIG, *Am I a Redundant Human Being?*

JOHN HAWKES, *The Passion Artist.*
Whistlejacket.

ELIZABETH HEIGHWAY, ED., *Contemporary Georgian Fiction.*

ALEKSANDAR HEMON, ED., *Best European Fiction.*

AIDAN HIGGINS, *Balcony of Europe.*
Blind Man's Bluff.
Bornholm Night-Ferry.
Flotsam and Jetsam.
Langrishe, Go Down.
Scenes from a Receding Past.

KEIZO HINO, *Isle of Dreams.*

KAZUSHI HOSAKA, *Plainsong.*

ALDOUS HUXLEY, *Antic Hay.*
Crome Yellow.
Point Counter Point.
Those Barren Leaves.
Time Must Have a Stop.

NAOYUKI II, *The Shadow of a Blue Cat.*

GERT JONKE, *Awakening to the Great Sleep War*
The Distant Sound.

GERT JONKE (cont.), *Geometric Regional Novel.*
Homage to Czerny.
The System of Vienna.
JACQUES JOUET, *Mountain R. Savage.*
Upstaged.
MIEKO KANAI, *The Word Book.*
YORAM KANIUK, *Life on Sandpaper.*
HUGH KENNER, *Flaubert.*
Joyce and Beckett: The Stoic Comedians.
Joyce's Voices.
DANILO KIŠ, *The Attic.*
Garden, Ashes.
The Lute and the Scars.
Psalm 44.
A Tomb for Boris Davidovich.
ANITA KONKKA, *A Fool's Paradise.*
GEORGE KONRÁD, *The City Builder.*
TADEUSZ KONWICKI, *A Minor Apocalypse.*
The Polish Complex.
MENIS KOUMANDAREAS, *Koula.*
ELAINE KRAF, *The Princess of 72nd Street.*
JIM KRUSOE, *Iceland.*
AYSE KULIN, *Farewell: A Mansion in Occupied Istanbul.*
EMILIO LASCANO TEGUI,
On Elegance While Sleeping.
ERIC LAURRENT, *Do Not Touch.*
VIOLETTE LEDUC, *La Bâtarde.*
EDOUARD LEVÉ, *Autoportrait.*
Suicide.
Works.
MARIO LEVI, *Istanbul Was a Fairy Tale.*
DEBORAH LEVY, *Billy and Girl.*
JOSÉ LEZAMA LIMA, *Paradiso.*
ROSA LIKSOM, *Dark Paradise.*
OSMAN LINS, *Avalovara.*
The Queen of the Prisons of Greece.
ALF MAC LOCHLAINN, *Out of Focus.*
The Corpus in the Library.
RON LOEWINSOHN, *Magnetic Field(s).*
MINA LOY, *Stories and Essays of Mina Loy.*
J.M. MACHADO DE ASSIS, *Stories*

MELISSA MALOUF, *More Than You Know*
D. KEITH MANO, *Take Five.*
MICHELINE AHARONIAN MARCOM,
The Mirror in the Well.
A Brief History of Yes.
BEN MARCUS,
The Age of Wire and String.
WALLACE MARKFIELD, *Teitlebaum's Window.*
To an Early Grave.
DAVID MARKSON, *Reader's Block.*
Wittgenstein's Mistress.
CAROLE MASO, *AVA.*
LADISLAV MATEJKA &
KRYSTYNA POMORSKA, EDS.,
Readings in Russian Poetics: Formalist and Structuralist Views.
HARRY MATHEWS, *Cigarettes.*
The Conversions.
The Human Country: New and Collected Stories.
The Journalist.
My Life in CIA.
Singular Pleasures.
The Sinking of the Odradek.
Stadium.
Tlooth.
JOSEPH MCELROY, *Night Soul and Other Stories.*
DONAL MCLAUGHLIN, *beheading the virgin mary*
ABDELWAHAB MEDDEB, *Talismano.*
GERHARD MEIER, *Isle of the Dead*
HERMAN MELVILLE,
The Confidence-Man.
AMANDA MICHALOPOULOU, *I'd Like.*
STEVEN MILLHAUSER,
The Barnum Museum.
In the Penny Arcade.
RALPH J. MILLS, JR., *Essays on Poetry.*
MOMUS, *The Book of Jokes.*
CHRISTINE MONTALBETTI,
The Origin of Man.
Western.
OLIVE MOORE, *Spleen.*

NICHOLAS MOSLEY, *Accident.*
Assassins.
Catastrophe Practice.
Experience and Religion.
A Garden of Trees.
Hopeful Monsters.
Imago Bird.
Impossible Object.
Inventing God.
Judith.
Look at the Dark.
Natalie Natalia.
Serpent.
Time at War.

WARREN MOTTE, *Fables of the Novel:*
French Fiction since 1990.
Fiction Now: The French Novel in the
21st Century.
Oulipo: A Primer of Potential Literature.

GERALD MURNANE, *Barley Patch.*
Inland.

YVES NAVARRE, *Our Share of Time.*
Sweet Tooth.

DOROTHY NELSON, *In Night's City.*
Tar and Feathers.

ESHKOL NEVO, *Homesick.*

WILFRIDO D. NOLLEDO, *But for the*
Lovers.

FLANN O'BRIEN, *At Swim-Two-Birds.*
The Best of Myles.
The Dalkey Archive.
The Hard Life.
The Poor Mouth.
The Third Policeman.

CLAUDE OLLIER, *The Mise-en-Scène.*
Wert and the Life Without End.

GIOVANNI ORELLI, *Walaschek's Dream.*

PATRIK OUŘEDNÍK, *Europeana.*
The Opportune Moment, 1855.

BORIS PAHOR, *Necropolis.*

FERNANDO DEL PASO, *News from*
the Empire.
Palinuro of Mexico.

ROBERT PINGET, *The Inquisitory.*
Mahu or The Material.
Trio.

MANUEL PUIG, *Betrayed by Rita*
Hayworth.
The Buenos Aires Affair.
Heartbreak Tango.

RAYMOND QUENEAU, T*he Last Days.*
Odile.
Pierrot Mon Ami.
Saint Glinglin.

ANN QUIN, *Berg.*
Passages.
Three.
Tripticks.

ISHMAEL REED, *The Free-Lance*
Pallbearers.
The Last Days of Louisiana Red.
Ishmael Reed: The Plays.
Juice!
Reckless Eyeballing.
The Terrible Threes.
The Terrible Twos.
Yellow Back Radio Broke-Down.

JASIA REICHARDT, *15 Journeys Warsaw*
to London.

NOËLLE REVAZ, *With the Animals.*

JOÃO UBALDO RIBEIRO, *House of the*
Fortunate Buddhas.

JEAN RICARDOU, *Place Names.*

RAINER MARIA RILKE, *The Notebooks of*
Malte Laurids Brigge.

JULIÁN RÍOS, *The House of Ulysses.*
Larva: A Midsummer Night's Babel.
Poundemonium.
Procession of Shadows.

AUGUSTO ROA BASTOS, *I the Supreme.*

DANIËL ROBBERECHTS, *Arriving in*
Avignon.

JEAN ROLIN, *The Explosion of the Radiator*
Hose.

OLIVIER ROLIN, *Hotel Crystal.*

ALIX CLEO ROUBAUD, *Alix's Journal.*

JACQUES ROUBAUD, *The Form of a City*
Changes Faster, Alas, Than the Human
Heart.
The Great Fire of London.
Hortense in Exile.
Hortense is Abducted.

FOR A FULL LIST OF PUBLICATIONS, VISIT: www.dalkeyarchive.com

JACQUES ROUBAUD (cont.), *The Loop.*
  *Mathematics: The Plurality of Worlds
  of Lewis.*
  The Princess Hoppy.
  Some Thing Black.
RAYMOND ROUSSEL,
  Impressions of Africa.
VEDRANA RUDAN, *Night.*
STIG SÆTERBAKKEN, *Siamese.*
  Self Control.
  Through the Night.
LYDIE SALVAYRE, *The Company of Ghosts.*
  The Lecture.
  The Power of Flies.
LUIS RAFAEL SÁNCHEZ, *Macho
  Camacho's Beat.*
SEVERO SARDUY, *Cobra & Maitreya.*
NATHALIE SARRAUTE, *Do You Hear
  Them?*
  Martereau.
  The Planetarium.
ARNO SCHMIDT, *Collected Novellas.*
  Collected Stories.
  Nobodaddy's Children.
  Two Novels.
ASAF SCHURR, *Motti.*
GAIL SCOTT, *My Paris.*
DAMION SEARLS,
  *What We Were Doing and Where We Were
  Going.*
JUNE AKERS SEESE, *Is This What Other
  Women Feel Too?*
  What Waiting Really Means.
BERNARD SHARE, *Inish. Transit.*
VIKTOR SHKLOVSKY, *Bowstring.*
  Knight's Move.
  *A Sentimental Journey: Memoirs
  1917–1922.*
  Energy of Delusion: A Book on Plot.
  Literature and Cinematography.
  Theory of Prose.
  Third Factory.
  Zoo, or Letters Not about Love.
PIERRE SINIAC, *The Collaborators.*
KJERSTI A. SKOMSVOLD, *The Faster I
  Walk, the Smaller I am.*

JOSEF ŠKVORECKÝ,
  The Engineer of Human Souls.
GILBERT SORRENTINO, *Aberration
  of Starlight.*
  Blue Pastoral.
  Crystal Vision.
  Imaginative Qualities of Actual Things.
  Mulligan Stew.
  Pack of Lies.
  Red the Fiend.
  The Sky Changes.
  Something Said.
  Splendide-Hôtel.
  Steelwork.
  Under the Shadow.
W. M. SPACKMAN, *The Complete Fiction.*
ANDRZEJ STASIUK, *Dukla.*
  Fado.
GERTRUDE STEIN, *The Making
  of Americans.*
  A Novel of Thank You.
GWEN LI SUI (ED.), *Telltale: 11 Stories*
LARS SVENDSEN, *A Philosophy of Evil.*
PIOTR SZEWC, *Annihilation.*
GONÇALO M. TAVARES, *Jerusalem.*
  Joseph Walser's Machine.
  Learning to Pray in the Age of Technique.
LUCIAN DAN TEODOROVICI, *Our
  Circus Presents...*
NIKANOR TERATOLOGEN, *Assisted
  Living.*
STEFAN THEMERSON, *Hobson's Island.*
  The Mystery of the Sardine.
  Tom Harris.
TAEKO TOMIOKA, *Building Waves.*
JOHN TOOMEY, *Sleepwalker.*
JEAN-PHILIPPE TOUSSAINT,
  The Bathroom.
  Camera.
  Monsieur.
  Reticence.
  Running Away.
  Self-Portrait Abroad.
  Television.
  The Truth about Marie.

FOR A FULL LIST OF PUBLICATIONS, VISIT: www.dalkeyarchive.com

DUMITRU TSEPENEAG, *Hotel Europa*.
The Necessary Marriage.
Pigeon Post.
Vain Art of the Fugue.
ESTHER TUSQUETS, *Stranded*.
DUBRAVKA UGRESIC,
Lend Me Your Character.
Thank You for Not Reading.
TOR ULVEN, *Replacement*.
MATI UNT, *Brecht at Night*.
Diary of a Blood Donor.
Things in the Night.
ÁLVARO URIBE & OLIVIA SEARS, EDS.,
Best of Contemporary Mexican Fiction.
ELOY URROZ, *Friction*.
The Obstacles.
BUKET UZUNER, *I am Istanbul*
LUISA VALENZUELA, *Dark Desires and
the Others*.
He Who Searches.
PAUL VERHAEGHEN, *Omega Minor*.
AGLAJA VETERANYI, *Why the Child is
Cooking in the Polenta*.
BORIS VIAN, *Heartsnatcher*.
LLORENÇ VILLALONGA, *The Dolls'
Room*.
TOOMAS VINT, *An Unending Landscape*.
IGOR VISHNEVETSKY, *Leningrad*
ORNELA VORPSI, *The Country Where No
One Ever Dies*.
AUSTRYN WAINHOUSE, *Hedyphagetica*.
CURTIS WHITE, *America's Magic
Mountain*.
The Idea of Home.
Memories of My Father Watching TV.
Requiem.
DIANE WILLIAMS, *Excitability:
Selected Stories*.
Romancer Erector.
DOUGLAS WOOLF, *Wall to Wall*.
Ya! & John-Juan.
JAY WRIGHT, *Polynomials and Pollen*.
The Presentable Art of Reading Absence.
PHILIP WYLIE, *Generation of Vipers*.

MARGUERITE YOUNG, *Angel in
the Forest*.
Miss MacIntosh, My Darling.
REYOUNG, *Unbabbling*.
VLADO ŽABOT, *The Succubus*.
ZORAN ŽIVKOVIĆ , *Hidden Camera*.
LOUIS ZUKOFSKY, *Collected Fiction*.
VITOMIL ZUPAN, *Minuet for Guitar*.
SCOTT ZWIREN, *God Head*.